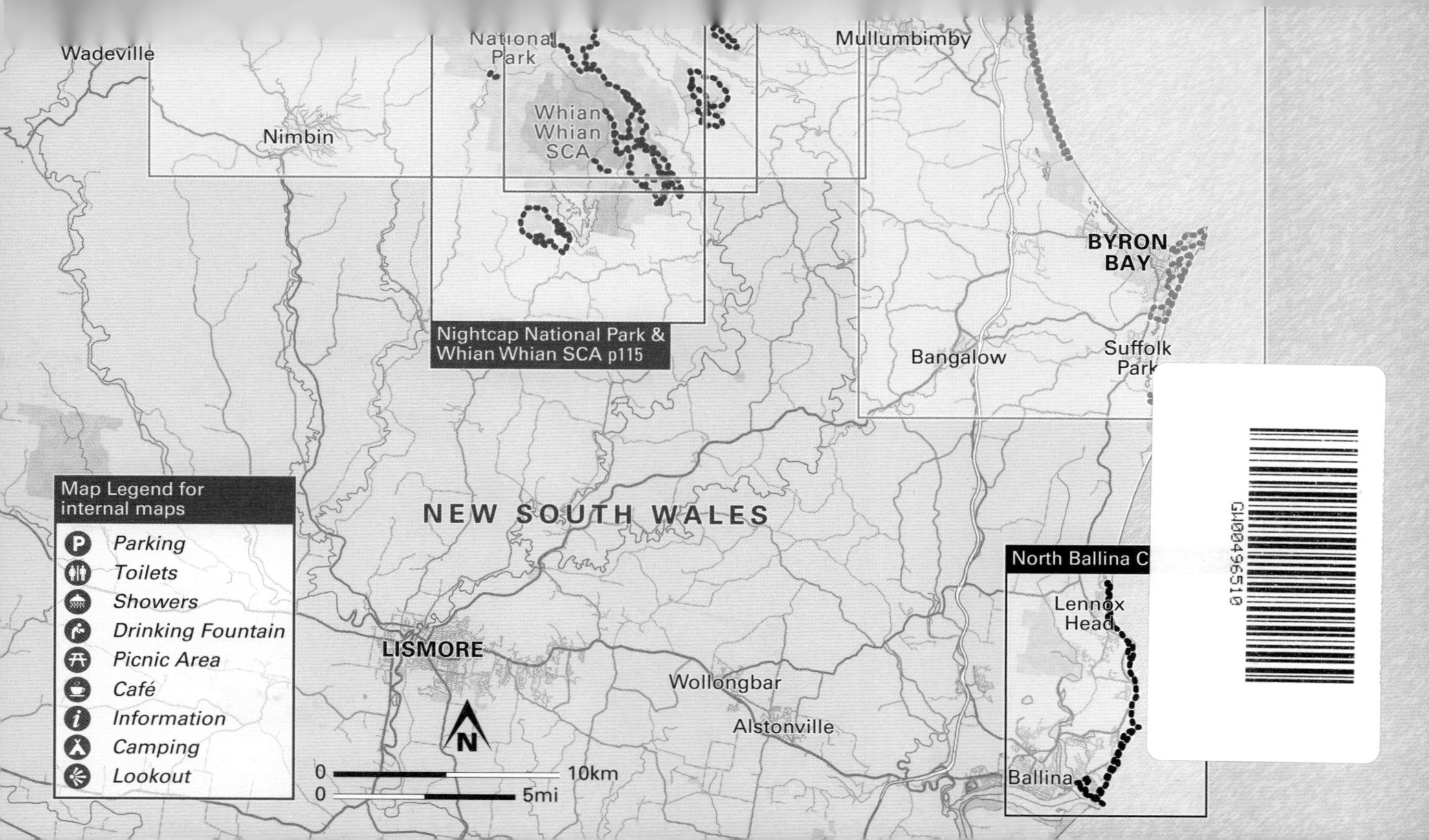

Wadeville
National Park
Nimbin
Whian Whian SCA
Mullumbimby
BYRON BAY
Nightcap National Park & Whian Whian SCA p115
Bangalow
Suffolk Park
NEW SOUTH WALES
Map Legend for internal maps
Parking
Toilets
Showers
Drinking Fountain
Picnic Area
Café
Information
Camping
Lookout
LISMORE
Wollongbar
Alstonville
N
0
10km
0
5mi
North Ballina C
Lennox Head
Ballina
GW00496510

Byron Trails

National Library of Australia Cataloguing-in-Publication entry

Cleary, Mairéad, author.

Byron trails : 50 walking adventures in Byron Bay and beyond / Mairéad Cleary.

9780994560100 (paperback)

Nature trails – New South Wales – Byron Bay Region – Guidebooks.
Walking – New South Wales – Byron Bay Region – Guidebooks.
Byron Bay Region (N.S.W.) – Guidebooks.

919.9443

Front cover photo by Dave Hall
Back cover photos by Tony White and Sera Wright
Front cover design by Kellie Knight
Internal design by Kellie Knight and Natalie Winter
Maps by Wayne Murphy

Printed in China by Everbest.

5 4 3 2 1 16 17 18 19 20

Byron Trails

50 walking adventures in Byron Bay and beyond

MAIRÉAD CLEARY

SPONSORED BY:

Contents

TWEED HINTERLAND

NORTH BALLINA COAST

NIGHTCAP NATIONAL PARK & WHIAN WHIAN SCA

Acknowledgements

Firstly I would like to acknowledge the Bundjalung people who are the traditional custodians of the lands mentioned in this book. I would also like to pay respect to the elders past and present of the Bundjalung Nation and extend that respect to other Aboriginal people.

There are many people who helped to make this book happen. Thank you Roz Hopkins and Natalie Winter at Captain Honey for your exceptional professionalism and sound advice. Many thanks to Kellie Knight for design, Bridget Blair for editing, Wayne Murphy for maps and the numerous photographers whose images adorn this book. I am deeply grateful to family and friends who supported me in this lengthy process, my beloved Samved for your constant strength, my family for your eternal generosity and love, and Michelle, Thirak and Mutribo for your encouragement and support. Thank you to Ian Fox, Jay Kearney and the many people who contributed their knowledge of walks in the area. Much gratitude to the following people for their valuable time: Ashley Moran, Bertha Kapeen, Dave Brown, Delta Kay, Gavin Brown, Leweena Williams, Marcus Ferguson, Michael Smith and Wayne Mukgrrngal Armytage. And last but certainly not least, thank you to the formidable Pozible supporters (Bob Brown and Michael Balson), sponsors (blk superwater, Crystal Castle, Santos Organics and The Bay Retreats) and 236 pledgers who generously helped to make this book happen.

To today's and tomorrow's lovers of nature and walking – this book is for you. May you experience first hand the delights and uncertainties of adventure.

Introduction

'What would our lives be like if our days and nights were as immersed in nature as they are in technology?' — RICHARD LOUV

With our busy modern times we are having less and less meaningful contact with nature in our day-to-day lives — to our detriment. Being in Nature is one of the best things we can do for our physical and mental health and wellbeing. It recharges us on so many levels.

Perhaps, like me, you have sometimes thought that Nature and its wildlife could be dangerous or threatening. Nothing could be further from the truth. Nature may be one of the last safe havens we have to turn to.

I've been lucky enough to have Nature around me most of my life, but taking up hiking in my mid-twenties was what led me to deeply appreciate its value. The sense of relaxation that Nature evokes is unsurpassable.

I've put this book together for people who have come to love Byron and its surrounds and for those lucky people discovering it for the first time. It offers all the essential information on walking trails in Byron and beyond and is bursting with hidden gems you probably didn't know existed.

It is my hope that this book brings you an experience of Nature that you will want to repeat again and again.

So go, explore, immerse and lap up what this beautiful area has to offer.

Mairéad Cleary, author.

Your Guide to Hiking

Advice to Readers

While the author has done her utmost to provide accurate information in this guide, your safety is your own responsibility. The information in this book is used at the reader's risk and no liability will be accepted for any personal injury, however incurred. The author makes no representation, undertakes no duty and accepts no responsibility to any third party who may use or rely upon the information, opinion or advice contained herein.

Hiking is a potentially risky activity. Make sure you are properly prepared before you go. Refer to the Hiking Know-How section for advice on what you'll need in the bush.

While this part of the world is very safe, it's always best not to leave valuables in your car when you go for a walk.

Facitilies Key

 **PARKING**

 **PICNIC TABLE**

 **TOILETS**

 **CAFE**

 **OUTDOOR SHOWER**

 **INFORMATION**

 **DRINKING WATER**

 **CAMPING**

How to Use This Guide

Inside the back cover you will find the trails listed by interest, length and level of difficulty. The Map Key on the inside of the front cover will give you an overview of the region and which map to refer to for your trail of interest.

Each trail has a level of difficulty rating from 'Easy' to 'Difficult'. This is based on distance, terrain and level of challenge involved.

You will find descriptions of the places to eat listed with each walk on page 161.

If you'd like someone else to figure out the navigation, or you'd just like to connect with other like-minded people, there are a range of outdoor guided tours in the area. A list of these is available on page 170.

Hiking Know-How

PLAN YOUR WALK

Be realistic about your physical ability and choose your trail based on what is manageable but also challenging for you. It's a good idea to choose a trail that will challenge you enough without overwhelming you.

Be prepared. Some of the national parks in this guide are in remote locations with little or no mobile reception. Carry suitable clothing and equipment, and advise family or friends of your walking plans, where you're going and when to expect you to return.

Know your walking speed. A relatively fit person walks an average of 5 kilometres per hour on flat level ground. That average drops to 4 kilometres per hour on uneven level ground. As the terrain climbs you'll need to add 10 minutes for every 100 metres of incline and with very steep inclines or declines you'll need to factor in more time again. In this guide the average time needed for each walk has been worked out for you. If you know yourself to be a slow walker however, allow extra time, particularly in winter when there is less daylight.

Note: Times indicated for each walk do not include side trips. Please allow extra time if you decide to do a side trip.

Stay informed. Check the weather before you go. If you are planning to walk in one of the national parks, check the Alerts section on the website of the New South Wales (NSW) National Parks and Wildlife Service (NPWS) for updates on the latest fires, floods and park closures. There is a link to NPWS

Alerts on www.byrontrails.com.

There are many helpful hikers and cyclists out there who flag unmarked junctions with pink or yellow ribbons to show the way. If in doubt, watch out for these ribbons.

Be Prepared – What to Wear

CLOTHES

Dress in layers so you can rug up or strip down according to the weather. Long lightweight breathable pants are best for the rainforest. Overheating and dehydration are important considerations in summer months. If you are prone to overheating you can buy 'cool hats' and 'cooling neck wraps' to help regulate your temperature.

HATS

Hats are an essential part of your walking gear in spring, summer and autumn. Grab one that's comfy and gives you the cover you need.

SHOES

Supportive shoes with a good tread are a must for most of the trails in this guide. Hiking shoes or sturdy runners will create minimal impact in ecologically sensitive areas, but which kind you need will depend on the walk you do. Runners are fine for the coastal walks. Once you wander into the rainforest you may need hiking shoes, which are sturdier than runners, are specifically designed for hiking and are usually waterproof.

Be Prepared – What to Bring With You

The equipment you need to take hiking with you will depend on the trail and will vary from necessary essentials to optional luxuries. Water is crucial for all walks.

ESSENTIALS

- About 2 litres of water for every 3 hours of walking (drink water before you leave too)
- Hat in spring, summer and autumn
- Snacks (fruit, nuts, trail mix)
- Electrolytes in summer
- Sunglasses
- Plastic bag for rubbish
- Warm layers in winter

LONGER TRAILS (3 HOURS +)

- Lunch
- Map and compass

- Swiss army knife
- Fully charged smartphone – in a ziplock bag
- Head torch (just in case)
- Whistle
- First aid kit
- Small ziplock bag to hold it all
- Some painkillers: paracetamol or stronger
- Ordinary and wide Band-Aids
- Pressure bandage for snake bite
- Small roll of sticky tape
- Tweezers for spikes and splinters
- Tea tree oil, or freeze spray (from a pharmacy) for tick removal
- Lighter or matches

OPTIONAL NON-ESSENTIALS

- Natural sunscreen – MooGoo is a good brand
- Natural insect repellent – Mosi-guard is the most effective natural insect repellant on the market and is available in health food stores and many outdoor camping stores
- Tissues
- Walking pole
- Camera
- Cool hat, cooling neck wrap in summer
- Moleskin pads to prevent blisters

If you plan to swim in any of the creeks along these trails it's best to avoid applying sunscreen or insect repellent and just cover up with light clothing.

Leave Only Footprints

Take only photos; leave only footprints. Take any rubbish, food scraps or tissues home with you. The ecosystems of many areas are extremely vulnerable and need all the help they can get. Please tread lightly.

Stay Out of Harm's Way

PLANTS

The main plants of concern on the trails in this guide are the giant stinging tree and wait-a-while vine. If you think you have been in contact with poisonous plants while hiking, take a hot soapy shower as soon as you get home.

Giant Stinging Tree

Giant stinging trees can be found in rainforest areas in the region such as Wollumbin National Park, Mt Jerusalem National Park, Nightcap National Park and more. The underside of the leaves, as well as the stems and fruit, are covered in tiny little hairs that inject neurotoxins into your skin producing an extremely painful sting. Look for large heart-shaped leaves with definitive serrated edges and white to red fruit that look like raspberries.

The effectiveness of various treatments is debatable. The sap of the cunjevoi plant, often found near to stinging trees, is reported to be an antidote. Paw paw ointment may provide some relief as it contains a protein digester. Sticky tape can at least remove the stinging hairs.

Wait-a-While Vine

Wait-a-while vine stems have prickly hooks that make the vine an excellent climber but will also grab hold of your clothes. There is only one way out of the vine and that is to stop and unhook yourself

piece by piece. You are only likely to encounter this vine when bush-bashing your way through an overgrown section such as the climb to the top of Mt Jerusalem.

INSECTS

The best prevention from insects and bugs when hiking is a good natural insect repellent. Be aware however that dosing yourself in repellent is also likely to repel the people walking behind you, as well as any wildlife that comes near you.

Leeches

Leeches love warm, wet conditions and thrive in subtropical rainforests. Use repellent on all bare skin, as well as on clothes and shoes. *Please note however that you should not spray repellant on your shoes if you are going into an ecologically sensitive area*. Leeches usually approach from the ground and can often be seen doing their own little hike up your shoe towards your juicy leg. For ultimate protection you can tuck your trousers into your socks and wear sock guards or gaiters over the top that have been sprayed with repellent.

There is no evidence that leeches transmit disease. In fact they are generally harmless. But it's a bit unpleasant to have one feeding on you, so what to do when you find one attached? The best way to deal with a leech is to flick it (which stuns it) and roll it off your skin. Keep rolling it between your fingers (which disorients it), then flick it into the bush.

Ticks

Ticks live on plants, trees and animals in low-lying bush and may climb on you as you brush past them. They cannot jump or fly. If you've walked through a heavily wooded or overgrown forest area check yourself for ticks afterwards. They are tiny creatures and you may only feel a small bump where

they have attached to your skin. It may itch.

There is a lot of conflicting advice about how to remove a tick. *Do not* pull it out with tweezers or fingernails. This is precisely the worst thing you could do, as it involves squeezing the tick or breaking its body, which may release poisonous fluids into your blood stream. Instead spray some tea tree oil or freeze spray on the tick (from your first aid kit). This kills the tick, a within a minute they should have released their grip and can be brushed off.

SNAKES

Snakes are more common in spring and summer, as they mostly hibernate during the colder winter months. Watch out for them in your path and wear long pants to protect your legs. The main advice to heed when it comes to snakes is to *leave them alone* and they will leave you alone. Most snakebites happen when people try to chase or handle them. You are unlikely to find brown snakes in the rainforest. They like open sunny ground and warm rocks.

If someone is bitten, send or phone for help to transport the person to hospital. *Don't* try to catch the snake for identification. Immediately apply firm pressure over the bite area. Lie the person down and keep them comfortable and still. Apply a pressure bandage (from your first aid kit) from the fingers or toes of the bitten limb upwards towards the body, including the joint above the bite site and as much of the limb as possible. Leave fingers and toes visible. Bandage firmly as if for a sprain, making sure that circulation isn't cut off. Bandage over clothes to minimise disturbance. Immobilise the limb with a splint (any rigid object) to prevent movement and try to include the joints above and below the bite.

About the Region

Weather

The Byron-Tweed-Ballina-Lismore area has a mild subtropical climate with hot, humid summers and mild, dry winters. Heavy rain can fall at any time of the year.

SPRING DAYS
(September–November) are warm and sunny (15–22°C).

SUMMER DAYS
(December–February) can bring hot, humid weather (25–30°C) with cloud, afternoon rains and occasional thunderstorms.

AUTUMN DAYS
(March–May) are generally warm (20–25°C) and wet.

WINTER DAYS
(June–August) are mostly glorious, clear, sunny days (10–20°C).

Getting Around

You will need a car or a bike to get around the region and to reach each of these walking trails.

Useful Telephone Numbers

Police/Fire/Ambulance: 000

SES assistance in floods and storms: 132 500

National Parks and Wildlife Service (NPWS): 13000 PARKS (13000 72757)

NSW Wildlife Information, Rescue and Education Service (WIRES) for injured wildlife: (02) 6628 1898

Nature as Medicine

'The outer world is necessary for the inner world. We need the sun, the moon, the stars, the rivers and the mountains and birds, the fish in the sea, to evoke a world of mystery, to evoke the sacred. It gives us a sense of awe.' — Thomas Berry

FEELING A BIT STRUNG OUT?

Studies reveal that spending time in a forest can ease stress and depressive symptoms and improve your sleep. Just being in nature, even for short periods of time, can reduce stress hormones and improve your immune defences. 'Forest bathing', as the Japanese call it, can have a long-lasting influence on our immune system's ability to resist invasions from harmful bacteria. With all these physical and mental health benefits, walking in nature becomes a perfect panacea. Nature simultaneously calms and focuses the mind, offering deep relaxation.

NEGATIVE IONS

Negative ions have also been shown to improve mood and to lessen stress, depression and anxiety, even reducing the incidence of panic attacks. You'll find an abundance of these little charged oxygen ions in forests and near moving water, and there are more of them in the air after rain or on clear, calm days and around sunrise and sunset.

GET THOSE HORMONES PUMPING!

Research shows that exposure to nature can lower blood pressure and reduce cortisol (the stress hormone). Being in nature also leads to higher levels of activity in the parasympathetic nervous system (the part responsible for calming us down) and increased serotonin production. Serotonin regulates our moods and is the hormone that strengthens and reinforces our human bonds. It is this hormone that antidepressant medications attempt to boost. Sunlight helps to produce serotonin in your body. The more sunlight you get, the more serotonin you produce. And exercise alters your serotonin production in similar ways to antidepressants.

After about three or four hours on the track your body starts to generate endorphins (also released by laughing), which give you a natural high.

The evidence is so sound that some mainstream health-care providers promote nature as therapy for all sorts of illnesses.

BECOME BRAINIER

The author Edith Cobb, an active observer of creative people and supporter of nature-based education, maintained that geniuses all share one interesting thing: a transcendent experience in nature in their early years. It seems that trees and plants give off aromas that affect our learning. Not only that, walking in the forest increases our levels of DHEA, a hormone that improves mental functioning. In fact researchers have shown that taking children into green areas improves cognitive function as much as the best ADHD medications do and that symptoms of ADHD reduce significantly when they are in nature.

The simple act of walking may be one of the most effective ways to protect your learning brain and keep fit. Spending hours in front of a screen has exactly the opposite effect, so the more high-tech we become, the more nature we need!

PROTECTING AGAINST NATURE-DEFICIT DISORDER

It seems that our civilised society may have completely underestimated how much the human brain is influenced by its physical environment and in particular by the natural world. Our attraction to and connection with nature may exist at the level of our DNA. As humans we need direct experience with nature.

In his book *Last Child in the Woods*, Richard Louv coined the phrase 'nature-deficit disorder' and described it as a diminished ability to find meaning in the life that surrounds us, whatever form it takes. By using this guide you are giving your children, your loved ones and yourself the gift of nature. The natural world is a treasure that connects you to your authentic self. It's the gift that keeps on giving, day after day in a myriad of ways.

As the pioneering naturalist and conservationist John Muir said, 'When we try to pick out anything by itself, we find it hitched to everything else in the Universe.'

Natural Environment

LANDSCAPE

The Byron-Tweed-Ballina-Nightcap area has a stunning landscape with a diverse mixture of vertical cliffs, pretty waterfalls, forest-covered slopes and agricultural land.

The most outstanding feature in the area is the majestic Wollumbin or Mt Warning. Wollumbin is the remnant core of the Tweed Volcano, which formed around 23 million years ago when this whole area was a volcanic hotbed.

Due to tectonic plate movement, the eastern perimeter of the Australian landmass was carried over a volcanic hotspot, causing the Tweed Volcano to erupt. This shield volcano was one of the most enormous in the ancient world. It poured basalt lava over the surrounding countryside, creating a massive lava dome over 2000 metres high (twice the height of Wollumbin today) and up to 90 kilometres in diameter! This outpouring carried on for three million years. The lava dome stretched from Lismore in the south to Tamborine in the north and from Kyogle in the west to Point Danger on the east coast.

The ranges that you now see surrounding Wollumbin, of which the Great Border Ranges and the Lamington Plateau are the most prominent, are the worn down remnants of this once great dome. The striking Tweed Pinnacle along the northwestern section of the Border Ranges marks the rim of the eroded crater.

As the volcano cooled and died and the basalt rock eroded under the forces of wind, water and rain, it left fertile basalt soil that was washed into the valleys below. Combined with high rainfall and warm subtropical climate, this created the perfect ground for rainforest, sclerophyll forest, woodland and coastal heath to grow and proliferate. The Big Scrub was born.

The more resistant rhyolite rock formed towering cliffs that today define the Tweed caldera. Minyon Falls in Nightcap National Park is a clear example of a rhyolite cliff. Wollumbin, the central core of the volcano, is made up mostly of erosion-resistant trachyandesite and syenite.

VEGETATION

Northeastern NSW supports the highest number of rare or threatened plant species in Australia and has as much native animal diversity as the wet tropics. This is mostly due to its location at an overlap between subtropical and temperate belts. In the warmer seasons low-pressure systems coming from the northern tropics cause torrential rain.

Rainforest, the oldest vegetation in Australia, once covered most of this area, as well as most of the Australian continent, in rich, shining green foliage. Today rainforest covers only about 0.25% of Australia.

We are lucky to have two World Heritage–listed Gondwana Rainforests of Australia closeby: Nightcap National Park and Wollumbin National Park. Gondwana Rainforests are considered natural treasures because they contain ancient plant and animal species whose origins can be traced back to the super continent, Gondwana.

The Big Scrub Rainforest

The Big Scrub rainforest that once covered northeastern NSW was the largest area of subtropical rainforest in Australia, covering an estimated 900 square kilometres. New York City by comparison covers 780 square kilometres. Of the original Big Scrub, less than 1% now remains. However significant remnants of lowland subtropical and littoral rainforest still exist. Littoral rainforest is considered one of the rarest types of rainforest in Australia.

Protestors Falls is named after the Terania Native Forest Action Group, who formed in 1979 to protest against logging in the area and to protect the rainforest of the Terania Basin. In fact were it not for this group of environmental activists, we would not have the publicly accessible treasure that is Nightcap National Park today. The action group of over 200 protestors peacefully obstructed logging operations in what became known as the Terania Blockade, the first major forest blockade in Australian history. The government at the time sent in the police to protect the loggers, rather than the rainforest (it appears that not much has changed today), but regardless logging was stopped in 1980 after months of protest.

After further protests, the NSW government finally declared the Nightcap Range a national park in 1982 and ultimately created Nightcap National Park in 1983 to include parts of Whian Whian State Forest. The blockade drew national attention and raised the question of rainforest protection throughout NSW and the rest of the country, with only 12% of original rainforest still intact in NSW alone. Fortunately the protests of Terania Creek were successful in bringing about the Rainforest Policy of October 1982 and the National Parks Preservation Act in 1983.

These days the local region supports subtropical, warm temperate, cool temperate, dry (semi-evergreen) and littoral (coastal) rainforest. What defines each type is the complex makeup of climate, soil, forest structure, leaf character and special life forms.

WILDLIFE

The Byron-Tweed-Ballina-Nightcap area has an abundance of wildlife, including scores of birds, mammals, reptiles and marine life.

Many birds are the propagators of seeds and the pollinators of flowers and help to disperse fruit seeds far from their original trees.

All levels of the rainforest provide a home for wildlife, from the thick leaf litter of the forest floor to the canopy above. Many animals have evolved through special relationships with certain plants and other animals, while some rely on a specific type of rainforest. Generally rainforest mammals are most active at night.

Native animals are extremely vulnerable to human interference. For this reason it's best to enjoy them from a distance. They are also vulnerable to injury in human environments such as roadways, drains and fenced areas. If you see sick or dead wildlife in the National Parks or Nature Reserves please report them to the ranger. If you cannot reach the ranger contact WIRES.

Please call WIRES on (02) 6628 1898 if you find sick or injured wildlife in the area.

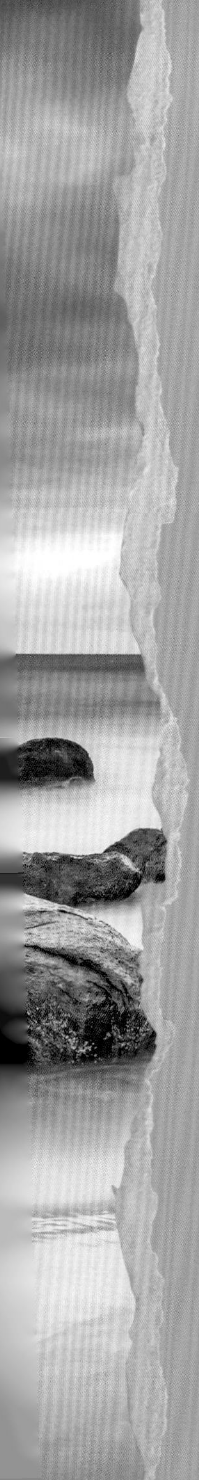

Byron Coast

NATURAL ENVIRONMENT

The most prominent coastal features on the Byron coast are Cape Byron, Julian Rocks and Broken Head. These formed due to the extensive folding of greywacke, slate, phyllite and quartzite metasediments; they are some of the oldest rock formations in the region (345–405 million years). The Broken Head Reserve is fringed by jagged, broken metamorphic rocks and sea stacks, and backed by steep folded slopes covered in subtropical rainforest.

Cape Byron supports low, windswept grasslands, including kangaroo grass on the exposed headlands such as at Little Wategos, as well as littoral and sclerophyll forests dominated by brush box and cabbage palm trees.

Just south of the cape, Arakwal National Park contains important habitat for many threatened plant species with intriguing names such as the stinking crypotocarya, the dark greenhood and the ground orchid. The park hosts a significant coastal heathland vegetation and wildlife corridor between Cape Byron and Lennox Head. Wallum heathland, in the elevated areas of the park, is the park's main vegetation.

Further south again Broken Head Nature Reserve supports a highly diverse native vegetation including some threatened and rare plant species. Littoral rainforest is the dominant vegetation in the reserve but you will also find dry sclerophyll forest, woodland, grassland and dunal vegetation. Also present are bangalow and cabbage tree palms, tree ferns, immense cycads, figs, and endless species of tropical plants.

North of the cape, Tyagarah Nature Reserve has patches of littoral rainforest, swamp sclerophyll forest, wet and dry heathland, as well as mangrove and saltmarsh along Simpsons Creek.

Further north again, Billinudgel Nature Reserve hosts a variety of forest and woodland including mature eucalypt forest, broad-leaf paperbark forest, scribbly gum, banksia woodland and coastal cypress pine. Melaleuca forest dominates. The reserve contains the largest intact remnant of swamp sclerophyll forest on the far north coast, making it an important coastal rainforest refuge.

With such a diversity of plant life, local, nomadic and migratory birdlife abounds. Coastal heath comes alive in spring with native birds and animals feasting on native blooming shrubs, bushes and grasses. In spring and summer nectar-eating birds such as the little wattlebird and noisy friarbird arrive for the local flowering. The growing, flowering and fruiting seasons of autumn and winter attract not just birds such as the golden whistler, regent bowerbird and brown gerygone, but also flying foxes and microbats. Fruit-eating birds and bats, such as the threatened grey-headed flying fox, are important for natural rainforest regrowth as they excrete the fruit's seeds as they move around.

Ospreys, brahminy kites and majestic white-bellied sea eagles patrol the coast, sometimes swooping dramatically to snatch food from the sea. Pied oystercatchers, with their distinctive long red beaks, may be seen searching for pipis along the beach.

Billinudgel Nature Reserve functions as a refuge for particular wetland fauna and fauna dependent on rainforest and old-growth forest. Wetland fauna include the laughing tree frog, comb-crested jacana, royal spoonbill, grass owl, little bronze-cuckoo and forest kingfisher. Rainforest fauna include the skink, flying fox, cuckoo-shrike, little shrike-thrush, varied triller and regent bowerbird. The old-growth forests are a scarce resource on the far north coast and provide food, den and nesting options for many species such as the koala, flying fox, square-tailed kite, glossy black cockatoo, masked owl and white-bellied sea eagle.

Larger fauna such as the greater glider and the grey kangaroo were once prevalent along the coast but have become locally extinct. However, the swamp wallaby population seems to be growing as vegetation regeneration matures. Other animals you may spot are the echidna, bandicoot, brushtail possum, tree snake, water dragon and goanna.

If you canoe, boat or paddleboard on Brunswick River, you might just see an endangered loggerhead turtle or a vulnerable green turtle coming up for air.

Cape Byron Marine Park off the coast supports several threatened species such as the humpback whale, the southern right whale, several species of turtle and the grey nurse shark. It also supports other species like dolphins. The elevation of Cape Byron and Broken Head makes them well placed for following the annual migration of humpback whales. Between 1954 and 1962 Cape Byron was a strategic site for directing whaling boats and due to their slow speed humpbacks were easy prey for the whalers. During that period the population of humpbacks along the eastern coast plummeted from 10,000 to approximately 100. Fortunately today they are protected in Australian waters and their numbers are increasing at about 11% per year. As of December 2015 their numbers are estimated at over 22,000.

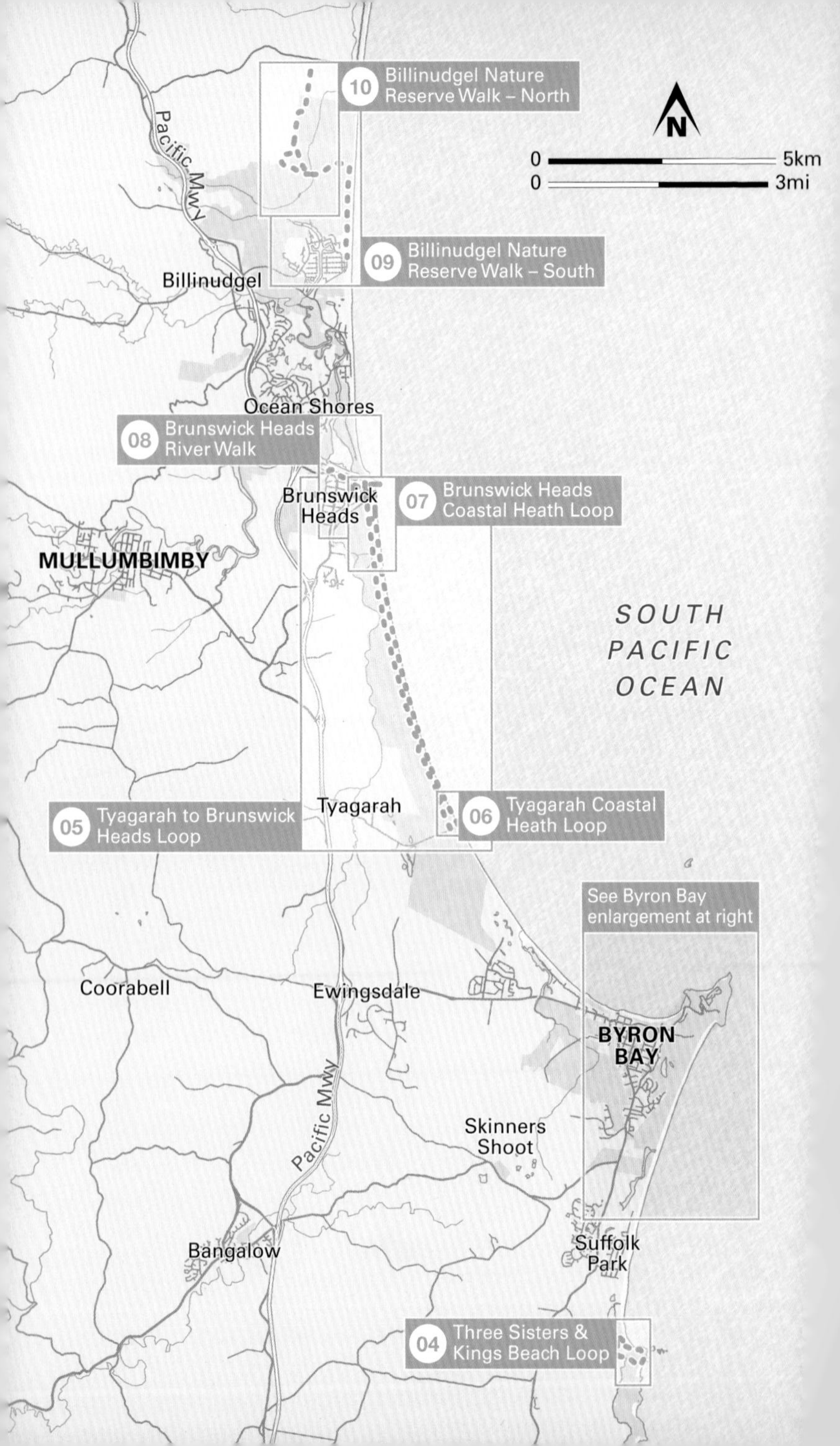

10 Billinudgel Nature Reserve Walk – North
0 5km
0 3mi
Pacific Mwy
09 Billinudgel Nature Reserve Walk – South
Billinudgel
Ocean Shores
08 Brunswick Heads River Walk
Brunswick Heads
07 Brunswick Heads Coastal Heath Loop
MULLUMBIMBY
SOUTH PACIFIC OCEAN
Tyagarah
05 Tyagarah to Brunswick Heads Loop
06 Tyagarah Coastal Heath Loop
See Byron Bay enlargement at right
Coorabell
Ewingsdale
BYRON BAY
Pacific Mwy
Skinners Shoot
Bangalow
Suffolk Park
04 Three Sisters & Kings Beach Loop

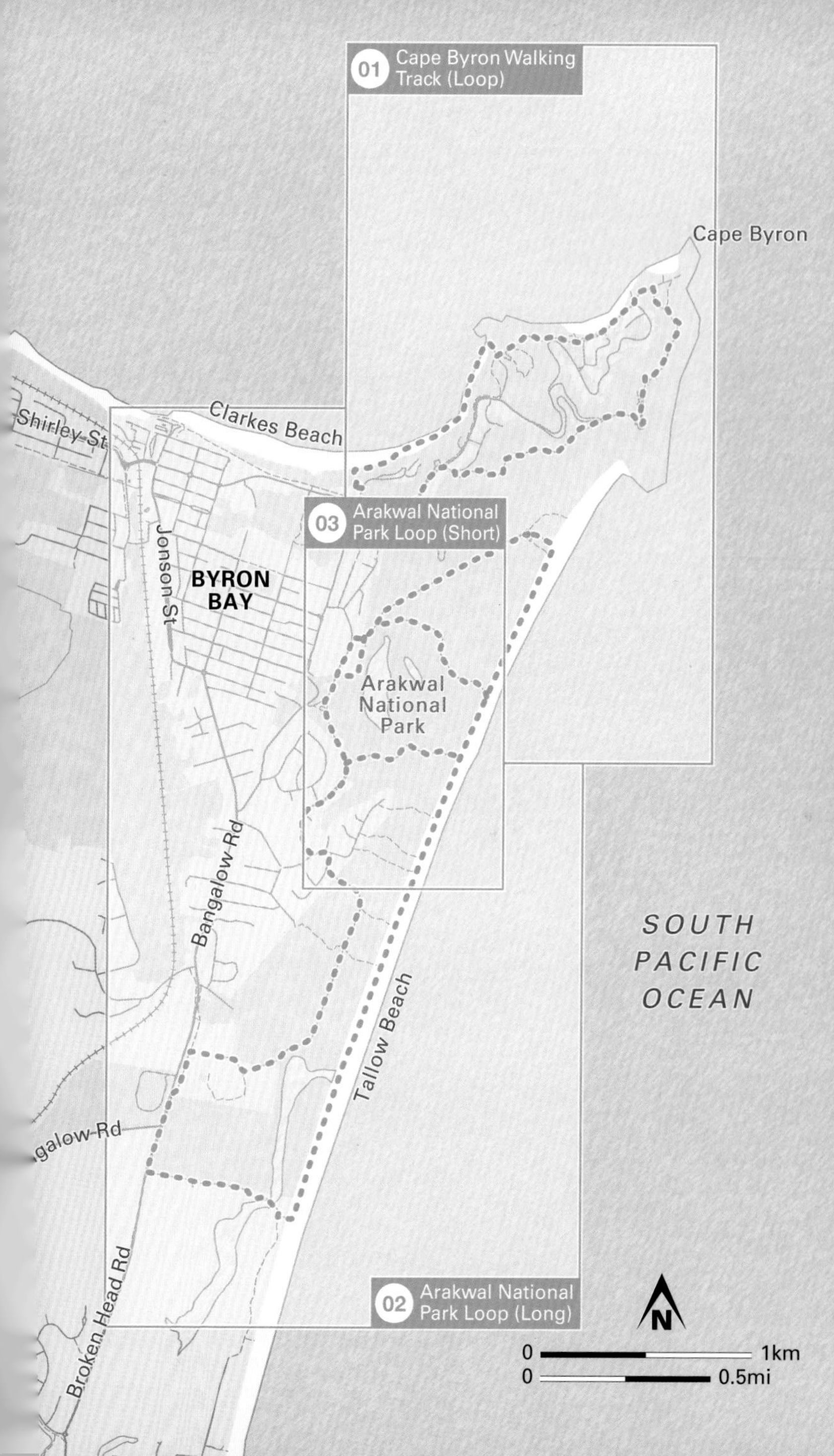
01 Cape Byron Walking Track (Loop)
Cape Byron
Clarkes Beach
Shirley St
03 Arakwal National Park Loop (Short)
Jonson St
BYRON BAY
Arakwal National Park
Bangalow Rd
SOUTH PACIFIC OCEAN
Tallow Beach
galow Rd
Broken Head Rd
02 Arakwal National Park Loop (Long)
N
0
1km
0
0.5mi

Cape Byron Walking Track
A Side Trip (A)
B Side Trip (B)

N
0 500m
0 0.25mi

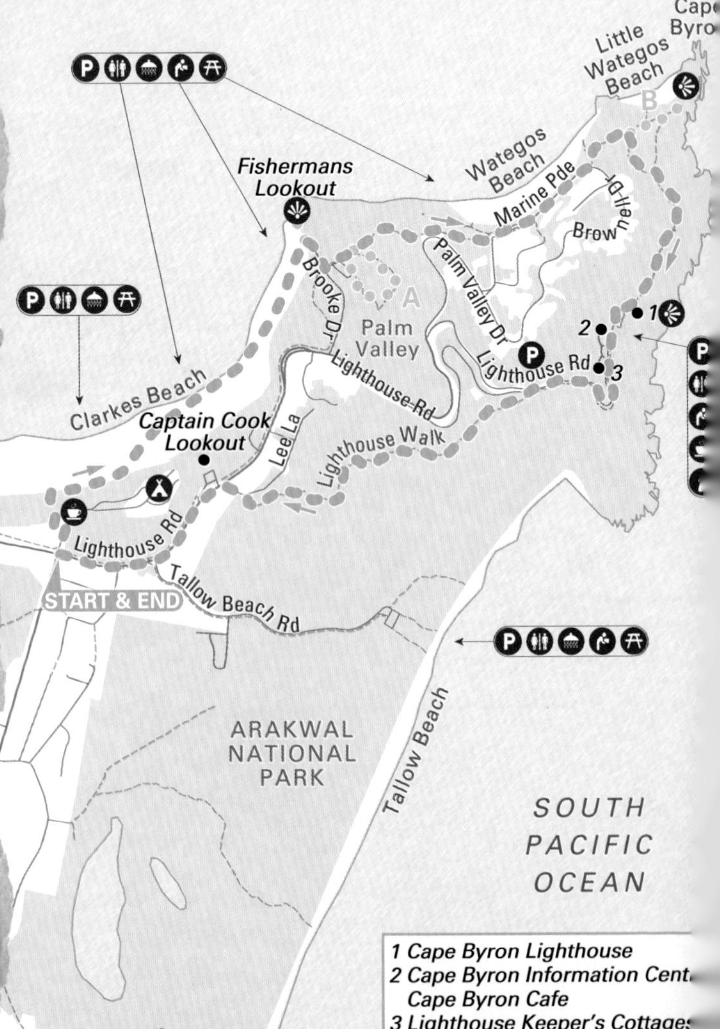

Expansive panoramic views and stunning beaches. Several viewing spots. May to October is whale season. Walking shoes recommended.

TRAILHEAD: Clarkes Beach car park

Follow the path down to the beach beside the Beach Café. Turn right and walk to Captain Cook lookout, identified by wooden steps up the steep outcrop. From there walk up the ramp to The Pass and veer left to pick up the paved track.

SIDE TRIP (A): ***A track breaks off to the right into Palm Valley and loops around to The Pass car park. Keep right to pick up the main track again.*** The main track climbs along an exposed cliff with the bay to your left, then drops down to Wategos Beach. Walk to the end of the beach then climb again along the headland to the lighthouse. SIDE TRIP (B): ***Steps lead left to Little Wategos Beach, which is a worthy diversion.*** This beautiful lighthouse area offers panoramic views up and down the east coast.

Continue downhill towards the Lighthouse Keeper's Cottages and the Cape Byron Information Centre, perhaps spending some time here and at the Cape Café. Follow the path along the railing taking in views of Tallow Beach and Broken Head, past a hang-gliding platform and into littoral rainforest. Emerging onto Lee Lane, walk downhill, cross the road and pick up the pedestrian path heading left and downhill, which takes you back to Clarkes Beach car park and completes the loop.

TERRAIN

Beach, paved path, forest track, steps and steep sections.

CHALLENGES

If walking this track around sunset, bring a torch for the rainforest section.

The Pass or Wategos Beach can have strong rips and currents.

GETTING THERE

Clarkes Beach car park is at the intersection of Lawson St and Massinger St.

CAFÉS

The Beach Café, The Pass Café, Cape Byron Lighthouse Café, Top Shop.

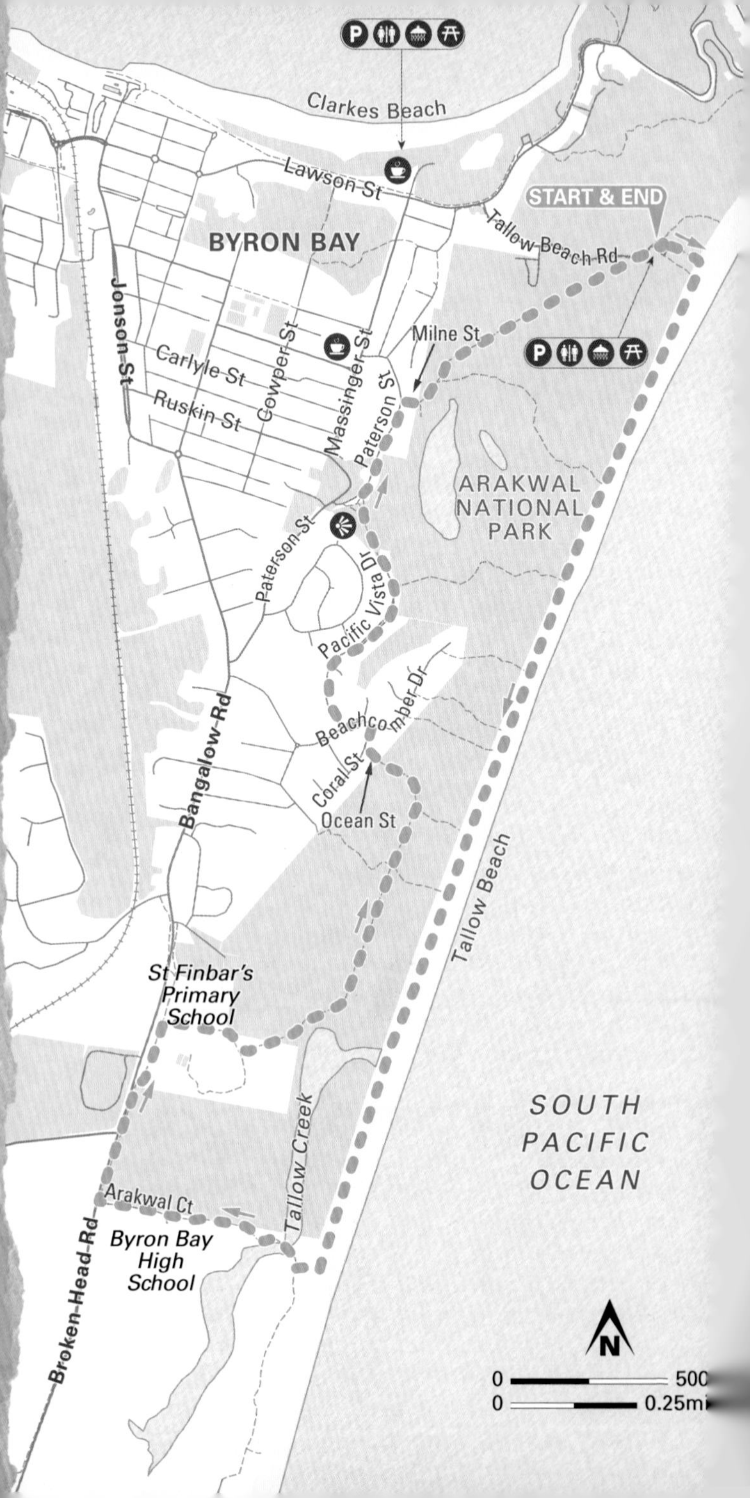

Clarkes Beach
Lawson St
START & END
Tallow Beach Rd
BYRON BAY
Jonson St
Carlyle St
Ruskin St
Cowper St
Massinger St
Milne St
Paterson St
ARAKWAL NATIONAL PARK
Paterson St
Pacific Vista Dr
Beachcomber Dr
Bangalow Rd
Coral St
Ocean St
Tallow Beach
St Finbar's Primary School
SOUTH PACIFIC OCEAN
Tallow Creek
Arakwal Ct
Byron Bay High School
Broken Head Rd
N
0 500
0 0.25mi

Panoramic coastal views, stunning beach and creekscapes. Walking shoes recommended.

TRAILHEAD: Cosy Corner car park

Access Tallow Beach, then turn right (south). After 40 mins Tallow Creek emerges on your right; soon after you reach an access point in the dunes that takes you inland. Turn right on the paved cycle path and follow it over the creek bridge, onto Broken Head Rd. Turn right and follow the pedestrian and cycle track to Byron Bay High School. Turn right and follow the road that runs between the high school and St Finbar's Primary School. The road becomes a track and skirts along the left of the high school fence until you pick up a fire trail to the left that takes you through the national park.

This track travels north parallel to the beach and eventually veers left onto Ocean St. From here take a right onto Coral Ct, a left on Beachcomber Dr and a right onto Pacific Vista Dr, which eventually becomes dirt track. Continue along this track. It offers some of the best views in Byron. At the end of the dirt track is a (shadeless) seating area.

Take a right onto Paterson St. After 300m take a right onto Milne St which takes you back into Arakwal National Park along a dirt track. After 800m you will reach Tallow Beach Rd. Take a right and follow the road to Tallow Beach car park.

TERRAIN

Beach, paved path, road and bush track.

CHALLENGES

Sun exposure in summer.

Very strong rips and currents along Tallow Beach; unpatrolled beach.

GETTING THERE

Cosy Corner car park is at the end of Tallow Beach Rd, off Lighthouse Rd.

CAFÉS

The Beach Café, The Pass Café, Top Shop.

03

Arakwal National Park Loop (Short)

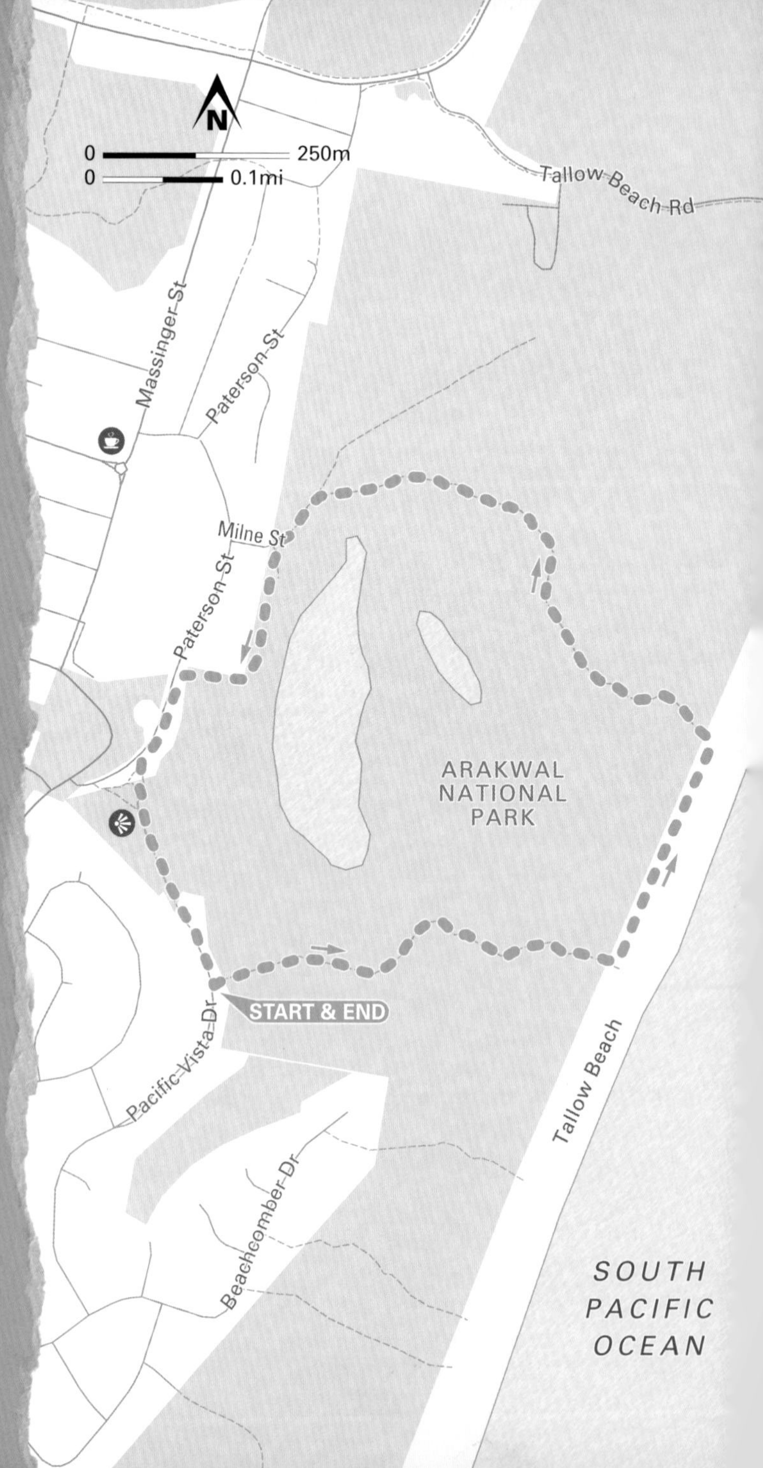

Nearest facilities: Byron Bay

Surprise views at various points along the track. Bird life abounds. Unique coastal rainforest.

TRAILHEAD: Arakwal National Park sign on Pacific Vista Dr

Take the track downhill from the sign. At one point you come to a semi-clearing. Veer diagonally to the left. Other than this the track is straightforward and takes you all the way to the beach. Turn left when on the beach and walk towards the cape and lighthouse. After 5 mins keep an eye out for a break in the vegetation which produces a sandy bank. You will mostly likely see footprints over the dunes at this point; follow them to a track through the coastal heath. You will pass some grass trees, coastal banksias (which attract abundant birdlife) and paperbark trees.

When you emerge onto a dirt road, turn left and walk towards Milne St. Rather than walk onto Milne St, keep walking along the edge of the national park as it skirts around the left of the houses. Follow the grassy verge uphill, walk through the gate and turn left. Walk briefly along Paterson St then take the dirt track to the left marked by another sign for the national park. There is a viewing bench here (shadeless) to take in the vast and stunning panorama of the cape and ocean. Continue along the dirt track to Pacific Vista Dr and the completion of the loop trail.

TERRAIN

Beach, path, bush track and road.

CHALLENGES

Watch for snakes along the narrow paths in summer.

GETTING THERE

Drive south from Byron Bay along Bangalow Rd. Turn left onto Patterson St, followed by a right onto Shelley Dr. Keep right to stay on Shelley Dr, turn right towards Pacific Vista Dr. Turn left onto Pacific Vista Dr.

CAFÉS

Top Shop,
The Roadhouse,
The Beach Café.

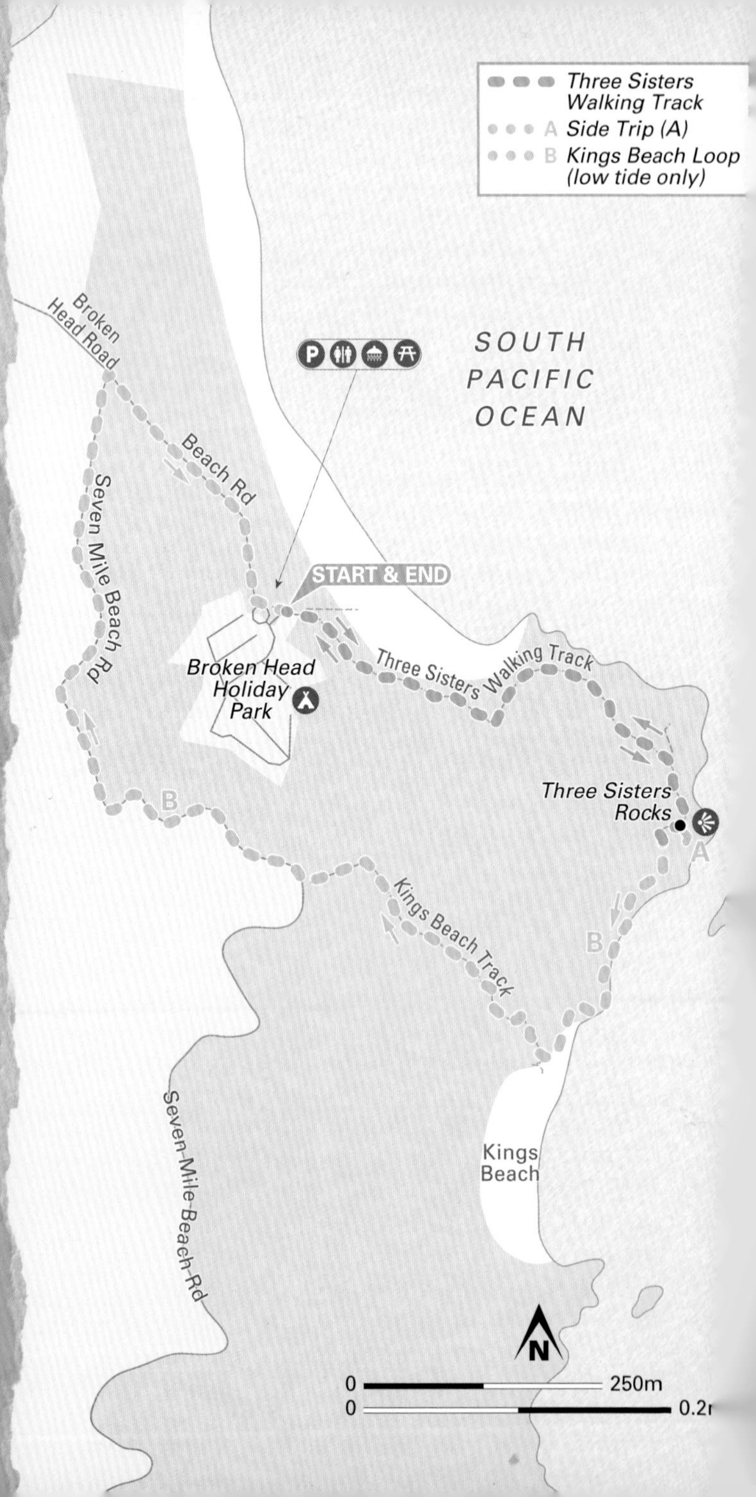

Three Sisters Walking Track
A Side Trip (A)
B Kings Beach Loop (low tide only)

SOUTH PACIFIC OCEAN

Broken Head Road
Beach Rd
Seven Mile Beach Rd
START & END
Broken Head Holiday Park
Three Sisters Walking Track
Three Sisters Rocks
A
B
B
Kings Beach Track
Kings Beach
Seven-Mile-Beach-Rd
N
0 250m
0 0.2

Two-part walk. Secluded, rocky beach coves and coastal rainforest. Winter and spring bring wildflowers.

NOTE: Kings Beach section can only be done at low tide. Check byrontrails.com for tides info

TRAILHEAD: Broken Head car park

Walking track (1.6km return, 45 mins): With the beach to your left, walk up the grassy hill. A sign marks the beginning of the track. The track takes you through littoral rainforest and under cottonwood canopy before it emerges to stunning coastal views north to Cape Byron. Continuing around the headland you will reach the Three Sisters rocks. An information board tells the Dreamtime story of the rocks.

SIDE TRIP (A): ***Just past the Three Sisters a stepped path leads left to a palm-covered rocky cove.***

As you walk further the headland opens up and offers expansive ocean views. At the viewing platform you can turn back and return along along the same track.

KINGS BEACH LOOP: To continue, take the stepped path beside the viewing platform to the rocky shore. Walk around the rocky outcrop to Kings Beach. From here steps lead up through stunning paperbark forest to Seven Mile Beach Rd. Turn right and walk 750m back to the intersection with Broken Head Rd. Turn right and return to the car park

TERRAIN

Coastal track, beach and unsealed road.

CHALLENGES

Sun exposure in summer.

Kings Beach is a 'clothes optional beach'.

The beach is isolated and unpatrolled and has numerous rips and rocks.

GETTING THERE

Broken Head car park is at the end of Broken Head Reserve Rd south of Byron Bay.

CAFÉS

The Roadhouse, Harvest Café.

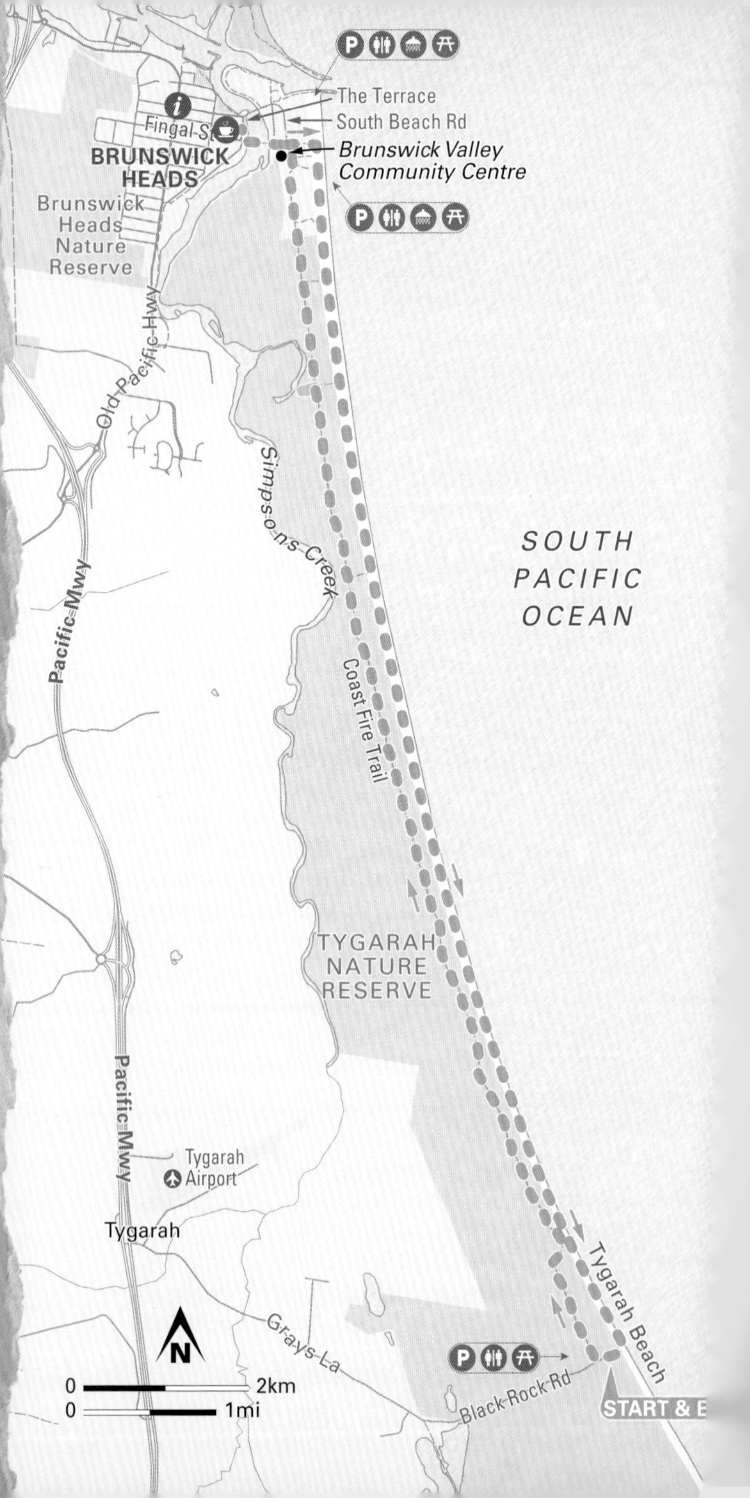

05

Tyagarah to Brunswick Heads Loop

The Terrace
South Beach Rd
Fingal St
BRUNSWICK HEADS
Brunswick Valley Community Centre
Brunswick Heads Nature Reserve
Old Pacific Hwy
Simpsons Creek
Coast Fire Trail
SOUTH PACIFIC OCEAN
Pacific Mwy
TYGARAH NATURE RESERVE
Tygarah Airport
Tygarah
Grays La
Black Rock Rd
Tygarah Beach
START & E

0 2km
0 1mi

Coastal heath, riverscapes, sea views.

NOTE: If you only want to walk one way leave one car in Brunswick Heads, then drive to Tyagarah to start.

TRAILHEAD: Tyagarah Beach car park

Walk back along the road from the car park for 100m to pick up the management trail on your right. After 5 to 10 mins the path curves right, then left, before straightening again. It then travels through coastal heath and forest for 7km.

There are two points along the management trail where you can turn off and walk inland to Simpson's Creek, a tributary of the Brunswick River, at 5km and 6km from the start of the trail. (Walking the other way, from Brunswick Heads, they are 1.3km and 2.4km from the start of the trail.) You can also access the beach at both of these points, along paths toward the coast.

The track ends at a reserve gate and emerges onto South Beach Rd (a good place to park if only walking one way). At this point you might want to turn left onto the pedestrian bridge after the Brunswick Valley Community Centre. The bridge takes you over Simpson's Creek to Brunswick's The Terrace and its cafés, and is a nice point to break.

Once revived, return along the bridge and cross the road to the beach. Turn right on the beach and walk south for 7.5km (1.5 to 2 hrs). The track to Tyagarah car park should be obvious due to footprints leading up and down the high dune. This completes the loop.

TERRAIN

Coastal heath track and beach.

CHALLENGES

Sun exposure in summer.

Tyagarah Beach is a designated 'clothes optional beach'.

Strong rips on Tyagarah and Brunswick beaches.

GETTING THERE

Grays Lane is accessed off the Pacific Highway 5km north of the Byron Bay highway entrance. Follow Gray's Lane (unsealed)to Tyagarah Beach car park.

CAFÉS

Brunswick Heads Cafés, The Farm.

06

Tyagarah Coastal Heath Loop

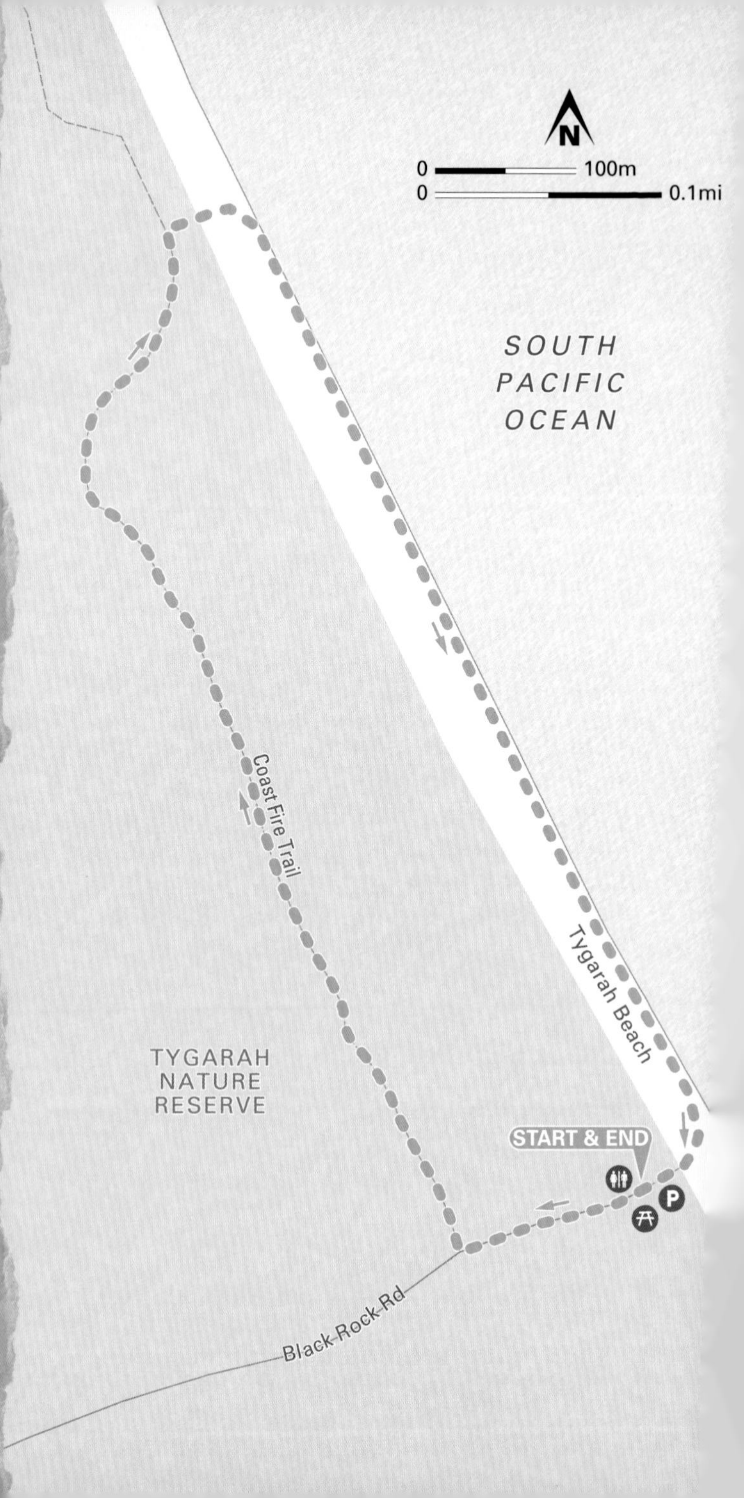

Starts in coastal heath and breaks onto pristine beach. A perfect morning refresher.

TRAILHEAD: Tyagarah Beach car park

Walk back along the road from the car park for 100m to pick up the management trail on your right. After approximately 5 to 10 mins the path curves to the right and then to the left. As the track straightens again you reach a track to your right through the heath. This track can be easy to miss so you will need to actively look out for it. This takes you to the beach. As you climb over the dunes, the ocean and beach beyond slowly come into view between the trees, which create a picture-perfect view frame, particularly on a sunny day.

On the beach turn right and walk south. Keep an eye out for the access track that marks the beach entrance/exit, easily identified by many footprints leading up along the high dune. This takes you back to the car park.

TERRAIN

Coastal heath track and beach.

CHALLENGES

Sun exposure in summer.

Tyagarah Beach has been designated a 'clothes optional beach'.

Strong rips.

GETTING THERE

Grays Lane is accessed off the Pacific Highway 5km north of the Byron Bay highway entrance. Follow Gray's Lane (unsealed)to Tyagarah Beach car park.

CAFÉS

The Farm.

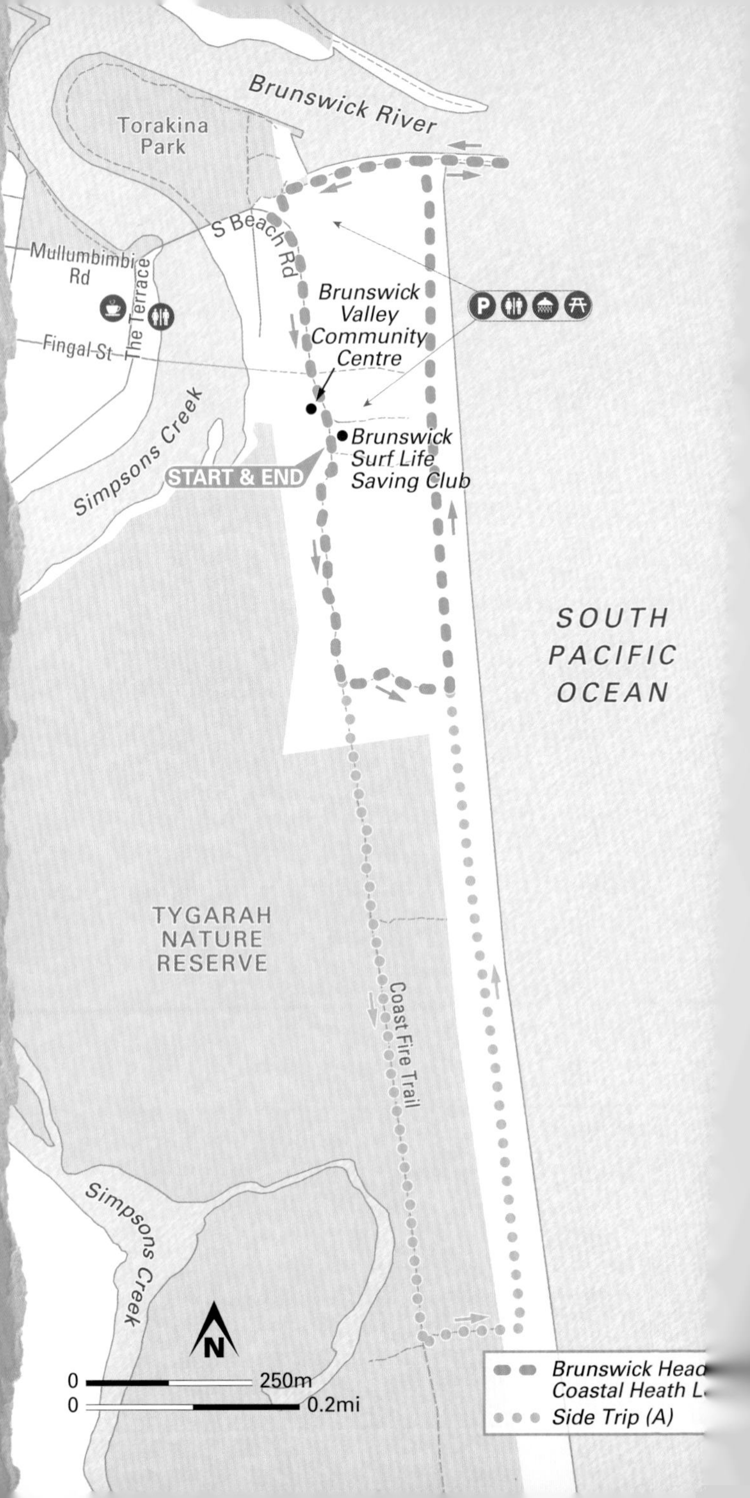

07

Brunswick Heads Coastal Heath Loop

Brunswick River

Torakina Park

S Beach Rd

Mullumbimbi Rd

The Terrace

Fingal St

Brunswick Valley Community Centre

Brunswick Surf Life Saving Club

START & END

Simpsons Creek

SOUTH PACIFIC OCEAN

TYGARAH NATURE RESERVE

Coast Fire Trail

Simpsons Creek

0 250m

0 0.2mi

Brunswick Head[s]
Coastal Heath L[oop]

Side Trip (A)

Easy walk that takes in costal heath, littoral rainforest and unspoilt beach.

TRAILHEAD: Brunswick Surf Life-Saving Club

Walk to the very end of South Beach Rd and go through the reserve gate. After 300m or 10 mins of walking in shaded forest you reach a second gate. Immediately after this there is a sandy track on the left that takes you to Brunswick Beach. Take this track.

SIDE TRIP (A): ***To extend your walk, continue 1 km to a four-way junction and turn left here.***

As you climb over the dunes, the ocean vista opens up between the trees, as does the panoramic beach view.

Turn left and walk north to the Brunswick River breakwall. Climb onto the breakwall and walk to the end. From here you get unique and picturesque views upriver towards Mt Chincogan in Mullumbimby. Follow the breakwall path to Torakina car park and turn left onto South Beach Rd to return to the surf life-saving club.

TERRAIN

Fire trail, beach and road.

CHALLENGES

Sun exposure in summer.

GETTING THERE

Brunswick Surf Life-Saving Club is at the end of South Beach Rd.

CAFÉS

Brunswick Heads cafés.

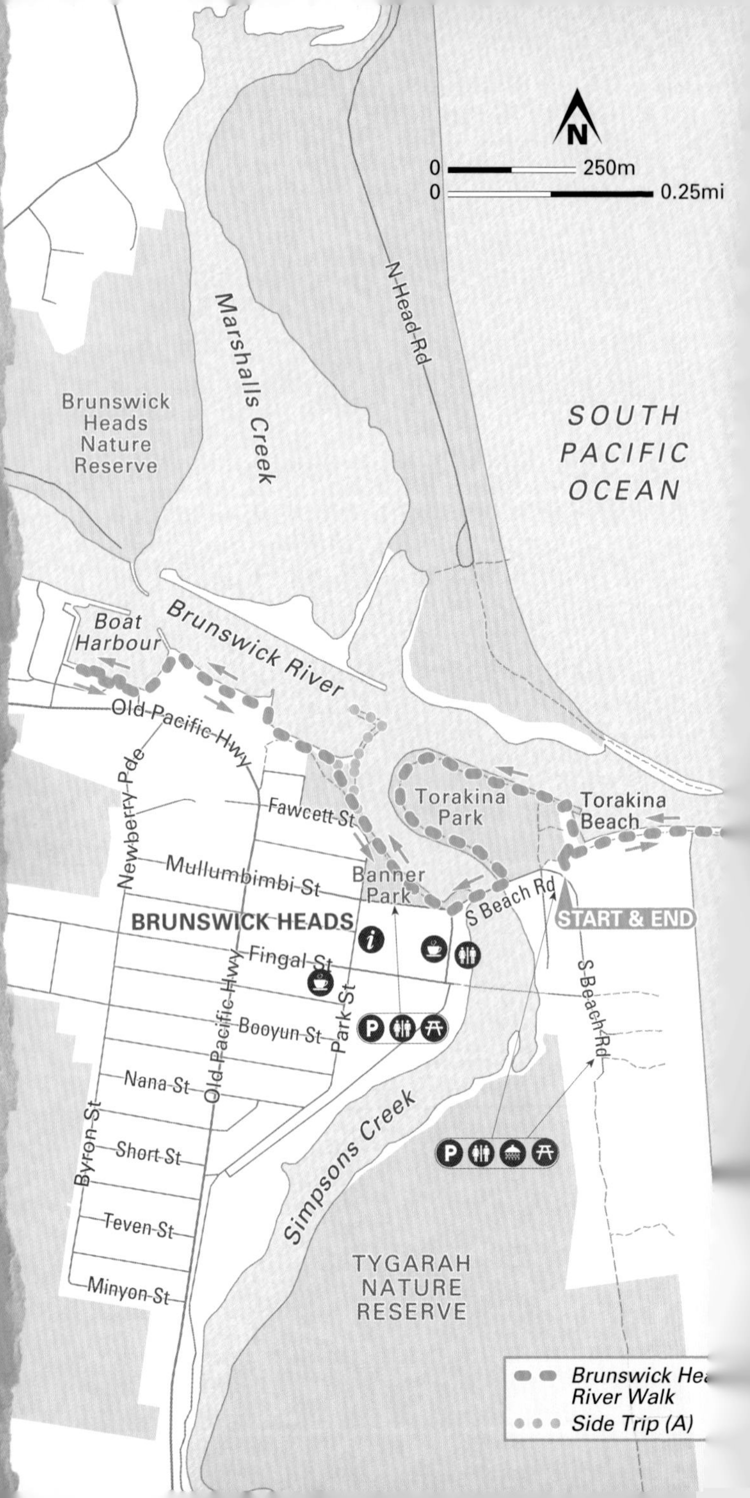

N

0 250m
0 0.25mi

Brunswick Heads Nature Reserve

Marshalls Creek

N-Head-Rd

SOUTH PACIFIC OCEAN

Boat Harbour

Brunswick River

Old-Pacific-Hwy

Newberry-Pde

Fawcett-St

Torakina Park

Torakina Beach

Mullumbimbi-St

Banner Park

S Beach Rd

START & END

BRUNSWICK HEADS

Fingal-St

S-Beach-Rd

Park-St

Booyun-St

Old-Pacific-Hwy

Nana-St

Byron-St

Short-St

Simpsons Creek

Teven-St

Minyon-St

TYGARAH NATURE RESERVE

Brunswick Hea
River Walk
Side Trip (A)

Takes in some of the best of the Brunswick Heads landscape – coastal heath, beach and river.

TRAILHEAD: South Beach Rd Parking Area

From the parking area and facilities veer right to walk along the river breakwall. The end of the breakwall offers unique views upriver towards Mt Chincogan in Mullumbimby.

Return along the breakwall path and turn right to cross the short stretch of Torakina Beach. Pick up the trail that leads off the beach onto the rocky riverside. The track almost loops back on itself and emerges just beside the wooden vehicle bridge.

Cross the bridge and keep to the right along the river. The informal track takes you past another breakwall where Brunswick River and Simpson's Creek meet.

SIDE TRIP (A): ***Consider taking the short walk out along the breakwall.***

Continue along the waterside to another, smaller breakwall and walk along the front of the North Coast Holiday Park. The path takes you to Brunswick Heads boat harbour.

Return the same way keeping the river to your left.

TERRAIN

Grass, path and road.

GETTING THERE

South Beach Rd runs from Brunswick Heads town towards the beach. There is parking all along the road.

CAFÉS

Brunswick Heads cafés.

09

Billinudgel Nature Reserve Walk – South

Toilets at Pacific Esp and Helen St junction

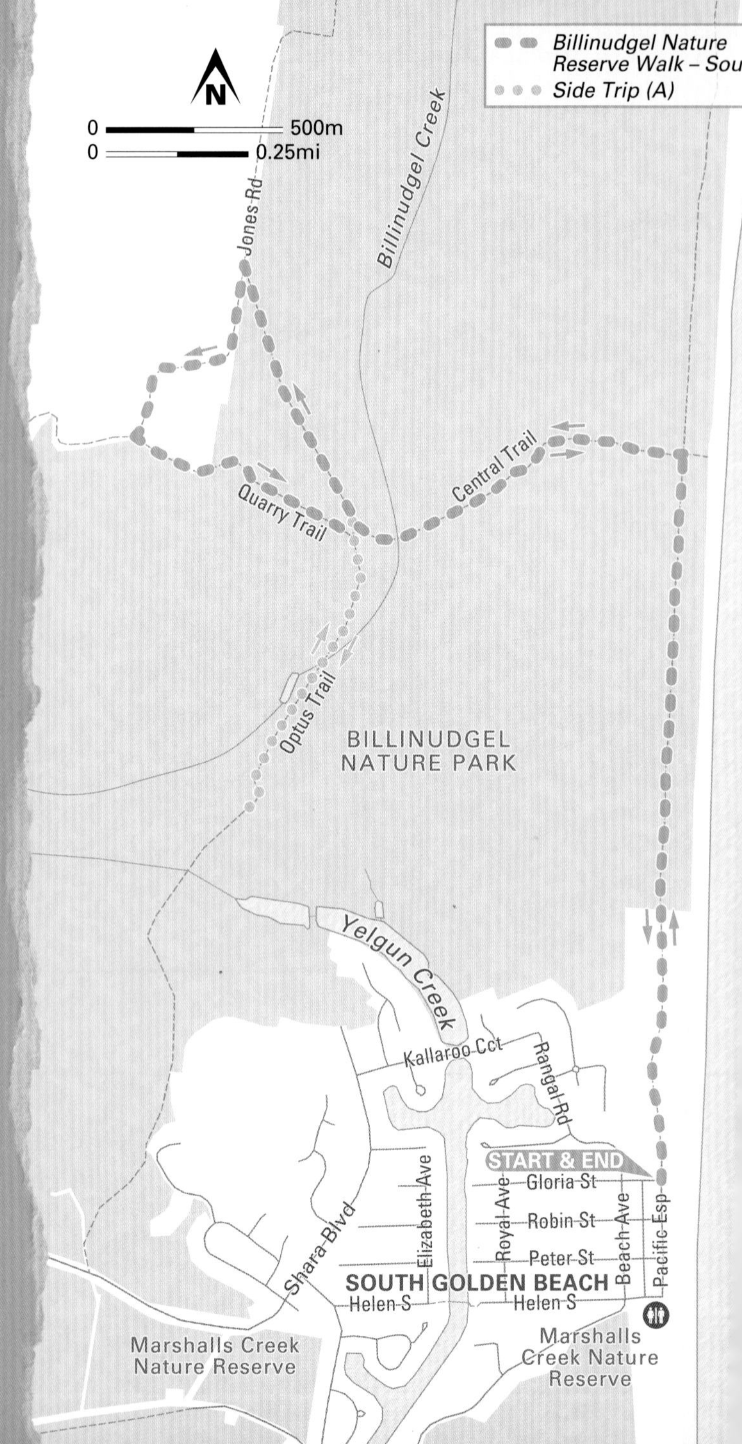

Peaceful nature walk through paperbark forest.

TRAILHEAD: Junction of Pacific Esp and Gloria St

From Pacific Esp walk north through the boulders onto the grassy Old Coast Rd track. After 10 mins turn right onto the dirt track. At the next junction (four-way) continue straight through the boulders. After 15 mins turn left onto Central Trail. The trail meanders through beautiful paperbark forest before reaching a junction where a small track veers to the right, followed immediately by a clearing and a three-track junction. Take the track to the right before the clearing.

After nearly 800m the track ends. If the grass is overgrown it can be hard to see Jones Rd, however walk through the grass towards the visible fence on your left and you will immediately find yourself on the road.

Turn left on Jones Rd. After 275m the road veers right and reaches a gate. Turn left to stay on Jones Rd. After about 150m is a left turn for Quarry Trail. Follow Quarry Trail for 700m before reaching the three-way junction and clearing again.

SIDE TRIP (A): *Walk along the Optus Trail for a while to experience picturesque paperbark track before doubling back to the Central Trai*l.

From here take Central Trail and retrace your steps to the Old Coast Rd. Turn right and return to Pacific Esp.

TERRAIN
Fire trails, path.

CHALLENGES
The Optus Trail can sometimes have water across it after heavy rain.

GETTING THERE
Pacific Esp runs parallel to the beach in South Golden Beach.

CAFÉS
Yum Yum Tree Café.

Nearest facilities: Pottsville and New Brighton

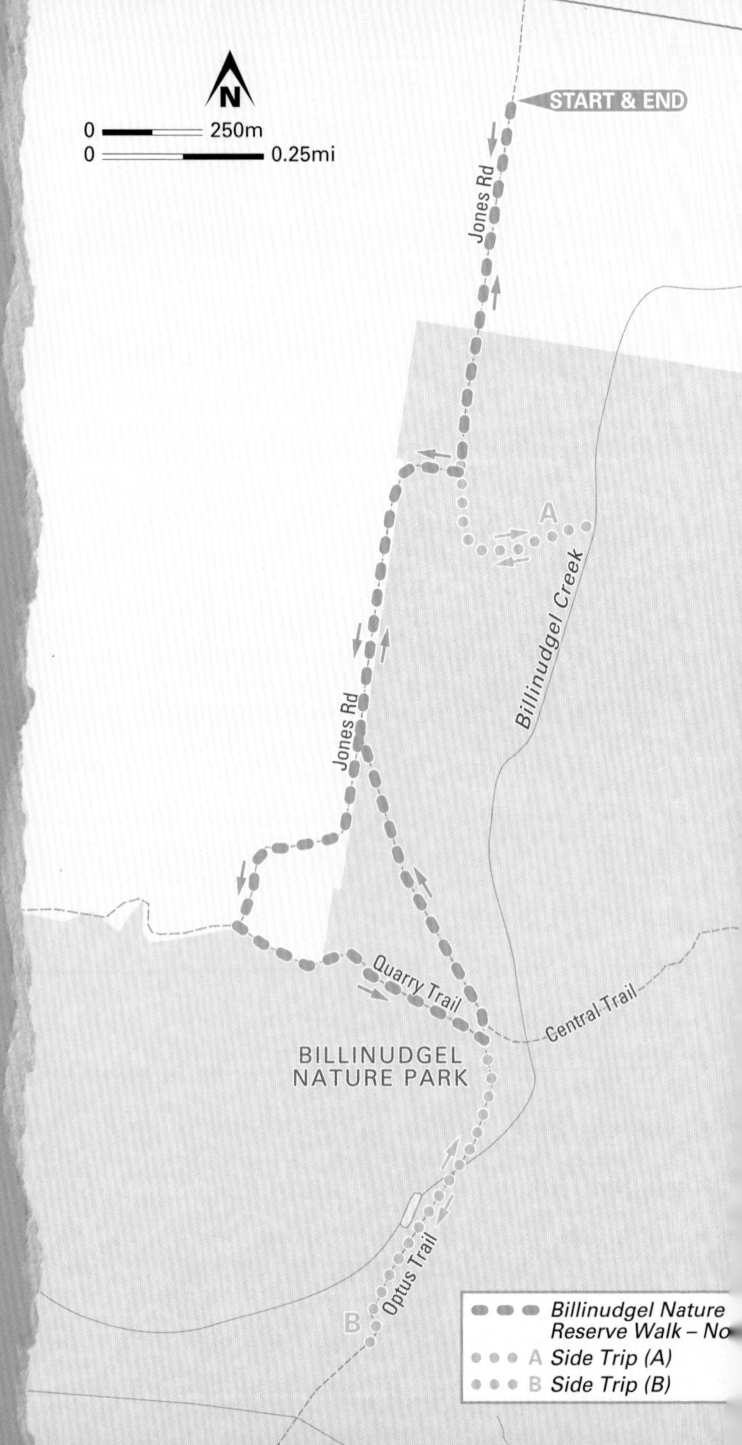

Peaceful nature walk through paperbark forest. Countryside views.

TRAILHEAD: Gate on Jones Rd

Walk through the gate on Jones Rd. After 500m go through another gate marking the northern boundary of the reserve. Some 350m along this road is a small track to the left marked by two boulders.

SIDE TRIP (A): *This smaller track meanders through mossy and picturesque woodland, eventually becoming overgrown and marshy.*

Another 150m along Jones Rd is a left turn at a private gate with a view across Wooyung farmland. Follow Jones Rd along the reserve's eastern boundary to another gate. Turn left after the gate to stay on Jones rd. After 150m turn left for Quarry Trail. Quarry Trail ends at a big clearing that serves as a three-track junction.

SIDE TRIP (B): *Walk along the Optus Trail (signposted) for a while to experience picturesque paperbark forest.*

From this clearing take Central Trail. Almost immediately along Central Trail is a track to the left. Follow this track nearly 800m to the end. If the grass is overgrown it can be hard to see Jones Rd, however walk through the grass towards the visible fence on your left and you will immediately find yourself on the road.

Turn right and follow Jones Rd back to your starting point.

TERRAIN

Fire trails, path.

CHALLENGES

The Optus Trail can sometimes have water across it after heavy rain.

GETTING THERE

Jones Rd is accessed from Wooyung Rd, which is accessed from Tweed Valley Way or the Tweed Coast Rd.

CAFÉS

Corner Stop Espresso Bar, Yum Yum Tree Café.

Byron Hinterland

NATURAL ENVIRONMENT

Goonengerry and Mt Jerusalem National Parks are part of the Tweed Volcano caldera. The original shield volcano, which has been substantially eroded, consisted mostly of basalt rock, while the ranges of Goonengerry and Mt Jerusalem National Parks are made up largely of the more erosion-resistant rhyolite. Burringbar Range, consisting mostly of phyllitic siltstone and shale extends from Mt Chowan in the southwest all the way to Mooball National Park in the northeast.

Goonengerry National Park was created in 1999 and covers 4.5 square kilometres. This small park is home to a variety of vegetation including flooded gum, tallowood, blackbutt, black she-oak and the rare syzygium hodgkinsoniae. The ridge is dominated by moist to dry sclerophyll forest and contains areas of old growth eucalypt forest, an important habitat for the threatened sooty owl. Other wildlife found in the park include the powerful owl, glossy black cockatoo, marbled frogmouth, Stephen's banded snake, monitor and koala.

Mt Jerusalem National Park was created in 1995 and covers 52 square kilometres. The park is home to warm temperate rainforest that has grown on rhyolitic soil and shares several plant and animal species with neighbouring Goonengerry. It lies within the Nightcap Range Important Bird Area as it has the largest known population of Albert's lyrebirds, as well as several other significant bird species. It is also home to a unique coral lichen and many rare and endangered plants such as symplocos baeuerlenii, syzygium hodgkinsoniae, tinospora tinosporoides, as well as various tree-dwelling animals and birds.

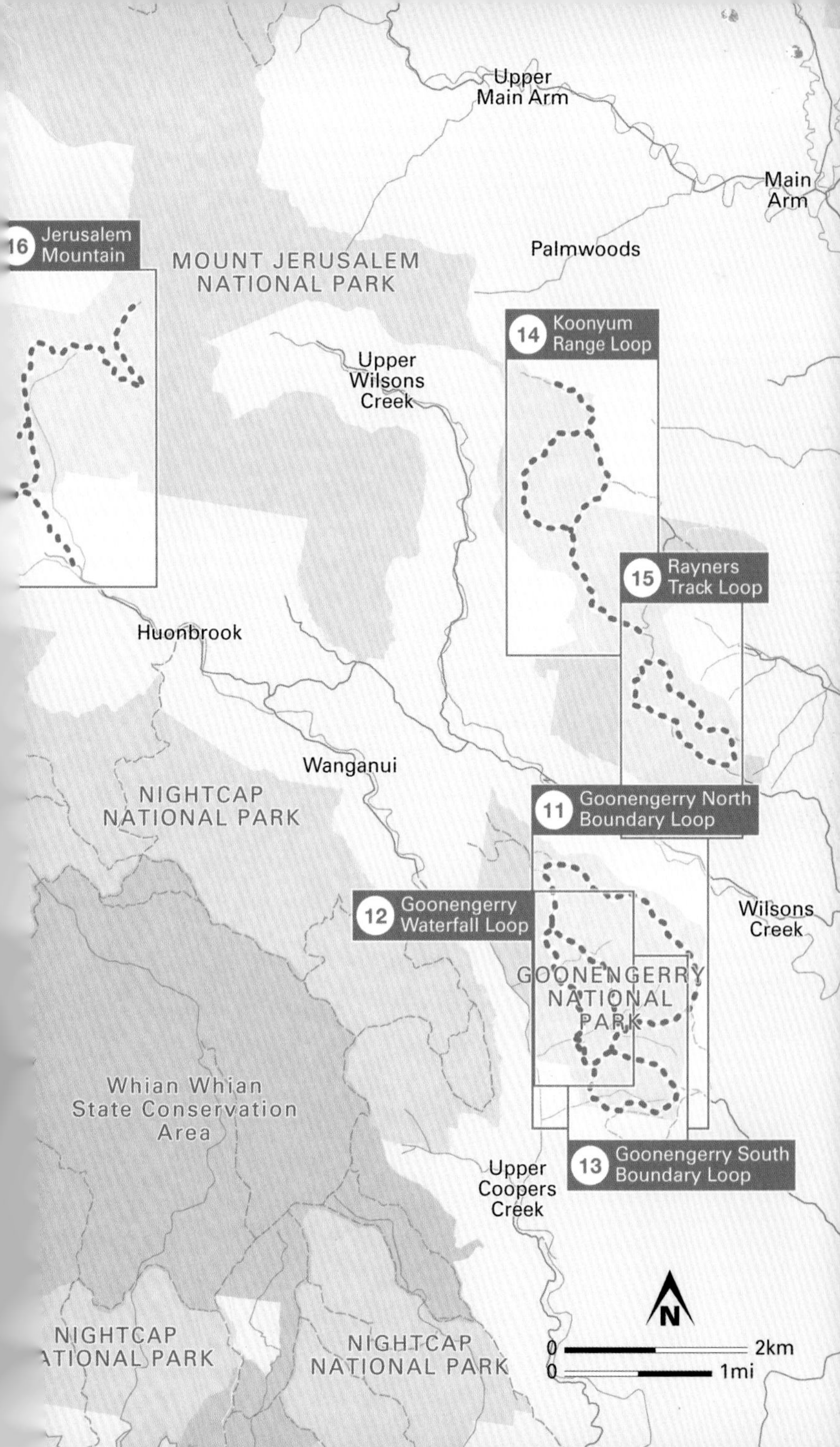
Upper Main Arm
Main Arm
Palmwoods
16 Jerusalem Mountain
MOUNT JERUSALEM NATIONAL PARK
14 Koonyum Range Loop
Upper Wilsons Creek
15 Rayners Track Loop
Huonbrook
Wanganui
NIGHTCAP NATIONAL PARK
11 Goonengerry North Boundary Loop
12 Goonengerry Waterfall Loop
Wilsons Creek
GOONENGERRY NATIONAL PARK
Whian Whian State Conservation Area
13 Goonengerry South Boundary Loop
Upper Coopers Creek
N
0 2km
0 1mi
NIGHTCAP NATIONAL PARK
NIGHTCAP NATIONAL PARK

11 Goonengerry North Boundary Loop

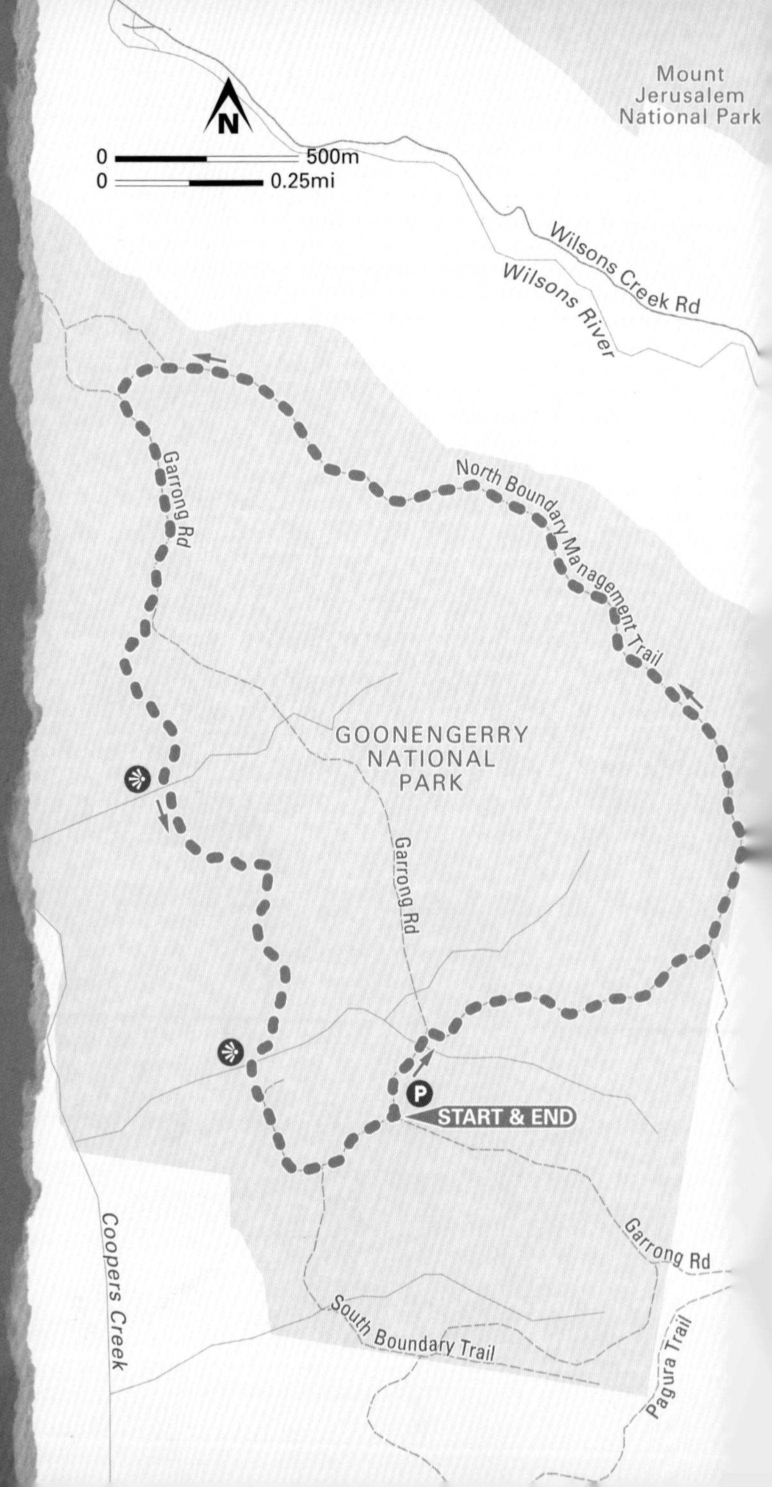

Nearest facilities: Federal and Mullumbimby

Takes in the periphery of Goonengerry National Park, two beautiful waterfalls and views across Wanganui Gorge to Nightcap National Park.

TRAILHEAD: Parking area on Garrong Rd

Walk through the northern gate (on right of parking area) onto Garrong Rd (unsigned). After 400m keep right for North Boundary Management Trail. The track ascends gradually eastwards to a crest and a fork. Keep left. The track veers north and crosses two creeks before climbing steadily to the northwestern corner of the park.

Keep left at the next two forks. You are now on Garrong Rd again. After 400m the road forks again. Take the right fork. The track descends steadily, then steeply southwards to a creek and waterfall that feeds Coopers Creek in the gorge below.

Directly across the creek the track continues south. It climbs steeply and is relatively rough and overgrown in parts. After the ascent eases you reach a junction. Turn right. After 350m ignore the small track to the left. At the next fork keep right. The track descends to another creek and waterfall.

Again, directly across the creek is a track leading southwards. The track forks almost immediately. Take either track as they converge further uphill. When you reach the big clearing and junction keep left. The track diverges again. Choose either path. Through the gate is the clearing where you parked.

TERRAIN

Fire trail, single track, some steep sections.

CHALLENGES

Lack of signage.

Overgrown track and fallen trees.

Leeches after rain.

GETTING THERE

Goonengerry Mill Rd is accessed off Goonengerry Rd just north of Goonengerry village. Just before Goonengerry Mill Rd enters the national park it becomes Garrong Rd.

CAFÉS

Crystal Castle, Doma Café.

12

Goonengerry Waterfall Loop

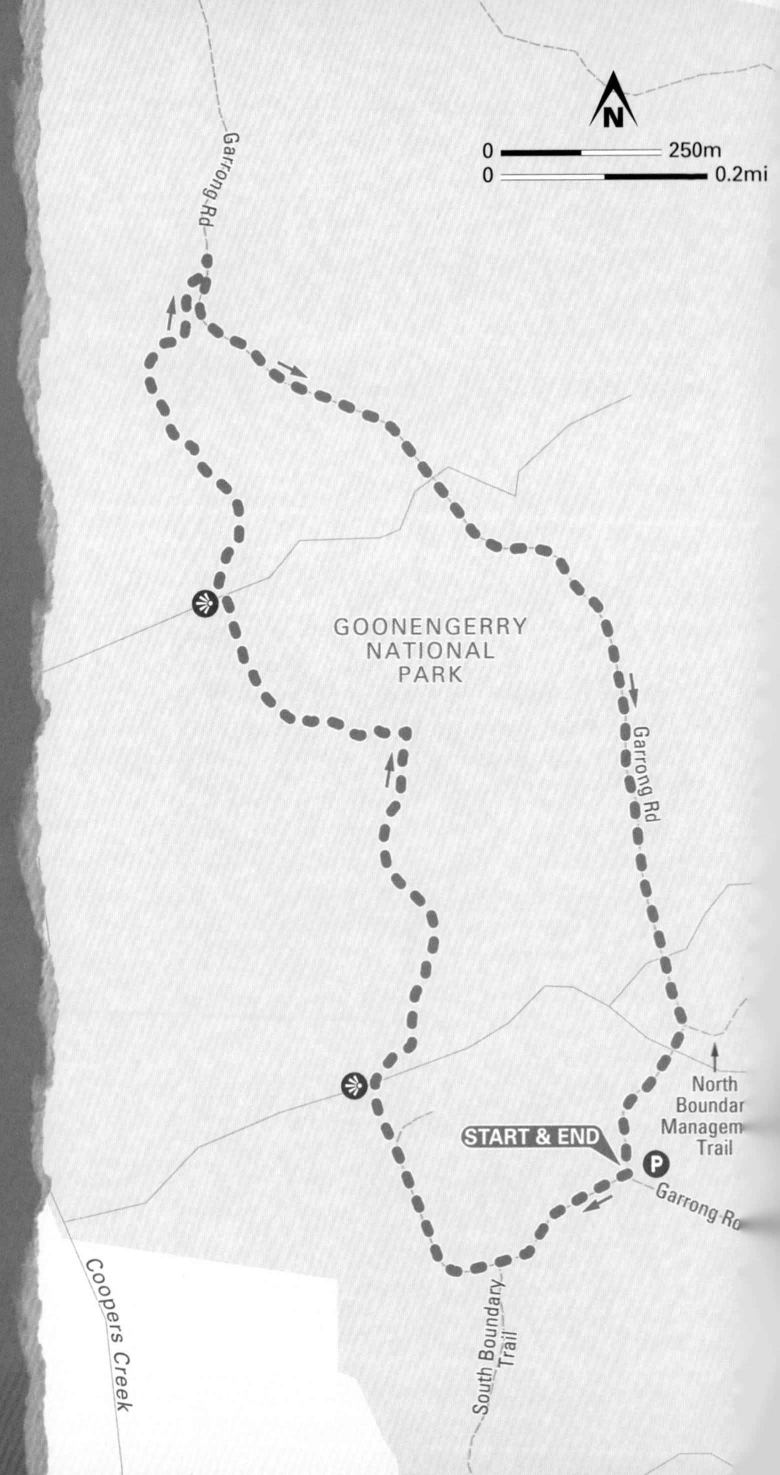

Nearest facilities: Federal and Mullumbimby

Beautiful forest and creekscapes with cliff-top waterfall views across Wanganui Gorge to Nightcap National Park.

TRAILHEAD: Parking area on Garrong Rd

Walk through the western gate (on far left of the parking area) onto the unsigned track. Keep right at the next two forks. Very soon you reach a large junction with an island of trees in the middle. Keep right and follow the track downhill. At the next fork keep left. The track descends for 300m to a creek tributary and waterfall that flows into Coopers Creek.

Directly across the creek is a track leading northwards. Follow this track uphill. From here the trail becomes overgrown but manageable. At the next fork keep left. After 150m ignore the small track to the right. After another 350m the track forks. Turn left. This section of the track is rough and descends gradually at first and then steeply to a second creek tributary and waterfall.

Again, directly across the creek is a track leading northwards from the creek. The track climbs steeply, then steadily northwards and eventually emerges onto Garrong Rd (unsigned). Turn sharp right onto Garrong Rd and enjoy the easy downhill stroll. The road climbs to a crest and a four-way junction. Continue straight. At the junction with North Boundary Management Trail, stay on Garrong Rd and cross the creek bridge. Through the gate is the clearing where you started your walk.

TERRAIN

Fire trail, single track, some steep sections.

CHALLENGES

Lack of signage.

Overgrown track and fallen trees.

Leeches after rain.

GETTING THERE

Goonengerry Mill Rd is accessed off Goonengerry Rd just north of Goonengerry village. Just before Goonengerry Mill Rd enters the national park it becomes Garrong Rd.

CAFÉS

Crystal Castle, Doma Café.

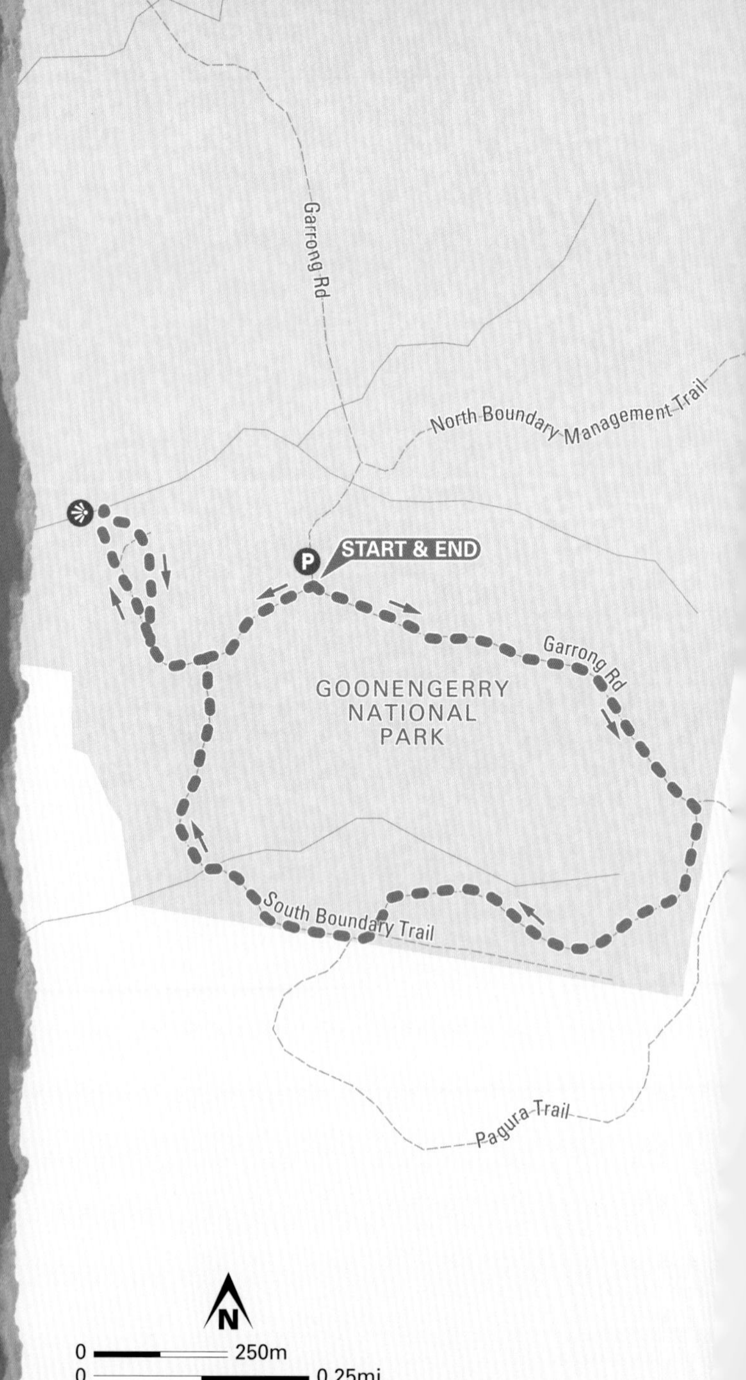
Garrong Rd
North Boundary Management Trail
START & END
P
Garrong Rd
GOONENGERRY
NATIONAL
PARK
South Boundary Trail
Pagura Trail
N
0
250m
0
0.25mi

Beautiful forest and creekscape with cliff-top view across to Nightcap National Park.

TRAILHEAD: Parking area on Garrong Rd

Walk back along the road you drove in by (Garrong Rd). After 850m the road forks. Keep right. Almost immediately the trail forks again. Keep right and walk through the gate. The trail descends steadily and heads south, then veers west through bangalow palm and brush box forest and reaches a clearing. The trail veers south again, then west and continues to descend. At another clearing the track turns right and descends to a tributary of Coopers Creek.

From the creek crossing the track climbs steadily northwards and reaches a four-way junction. To get to the waterfall, take a sharp left. Almost immediately is a large junction with an island of trees in the middle. Keep right. At the next fork keep left. The track descends for 300m to another Coopers Creek tributary and the creek waterfall. The waterfall offers views across Wanganui Gorge to Nightcap National Park and escarpment.

To return, retrace your steps from the creek. The track forks almost immediately. Keep left this time and climb steadily uphill to where the tracks converge again. When you reach the big clearing keep left. The track diverges again. Choose either path. Through the gate is the clearing where you parked.

TERRAIN

Fire trail, single track.

CHALLENGES

Fallen trees.

Sheer cliff edge at waterfall.

Leeches after rain.

GETTING THERE

Goonengerry Mill Rd is accessed off Goonengerry Rd just north of Goonengerry village. Just before Goonengerry Mill Rd enters the national park it becomes Garrong Rd.

CAFÉS

Crystal Castle, Doma Café.

14

Koonyum Range Loop

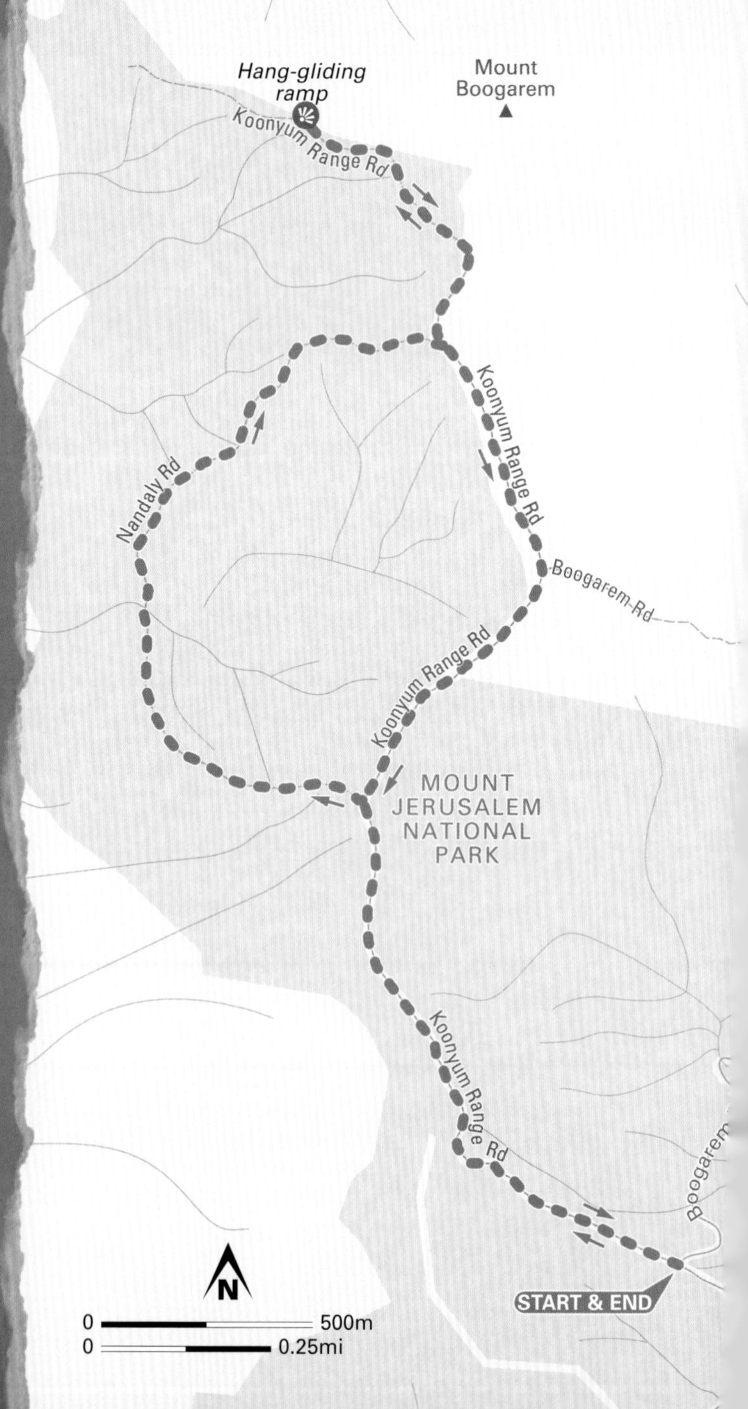

Nearest facilities: Mullumbimby

Views to Durrumbul and Upper Main Arm. Good summer walk due to higher altitude and tree shade.

TRAILHEAD: Intersection of Koonyum Range Rd and Boogarem Rd

At the junction of Koonyum Range Rd and Boogarem Rd keep left for Koonyum Range Rd. The trail climbs steadily along easy grade road. After 1.5km turn left onto Nandaly Rd (signposted and marked by a gate). The road gradually descends to a creek crossing and then climbs to meet Koonyum Range Rd. Turn left. After 220m the road forks. Keep left again. After 550m the track ends at a grassy hang-gliding ramp that offers extensive views over Durrumbul, Main Arm and Upper Main Arm.

Return along the same track, but continue straight past the right turn for Nandaly Rd. At the next junction (600m after Nandaly Rd), keep right to stay on Koonyum Range Rd. After 700m you return to the turn-off you initially took for Nandaly Rd. Continue along Koonyum Range Rd which now descends steadily taking you back to the junction with Boogarem Rd and completing the trail.

TERRAIN

Unsealed road, fire trail, single track.

CHALLENGES

Koonyum Range Rd can be slippery when wet.

GETTING THERE

Koonyum Range Rd is accessed from Wilson's Creek Rd to the southwest of Mullumbimby. It is unsealed. The intersection with Boogarem Rd is 2.6km from the entrance to Mt Jerusalem National Park.

CAFÉS

Mullumbimby cafés.

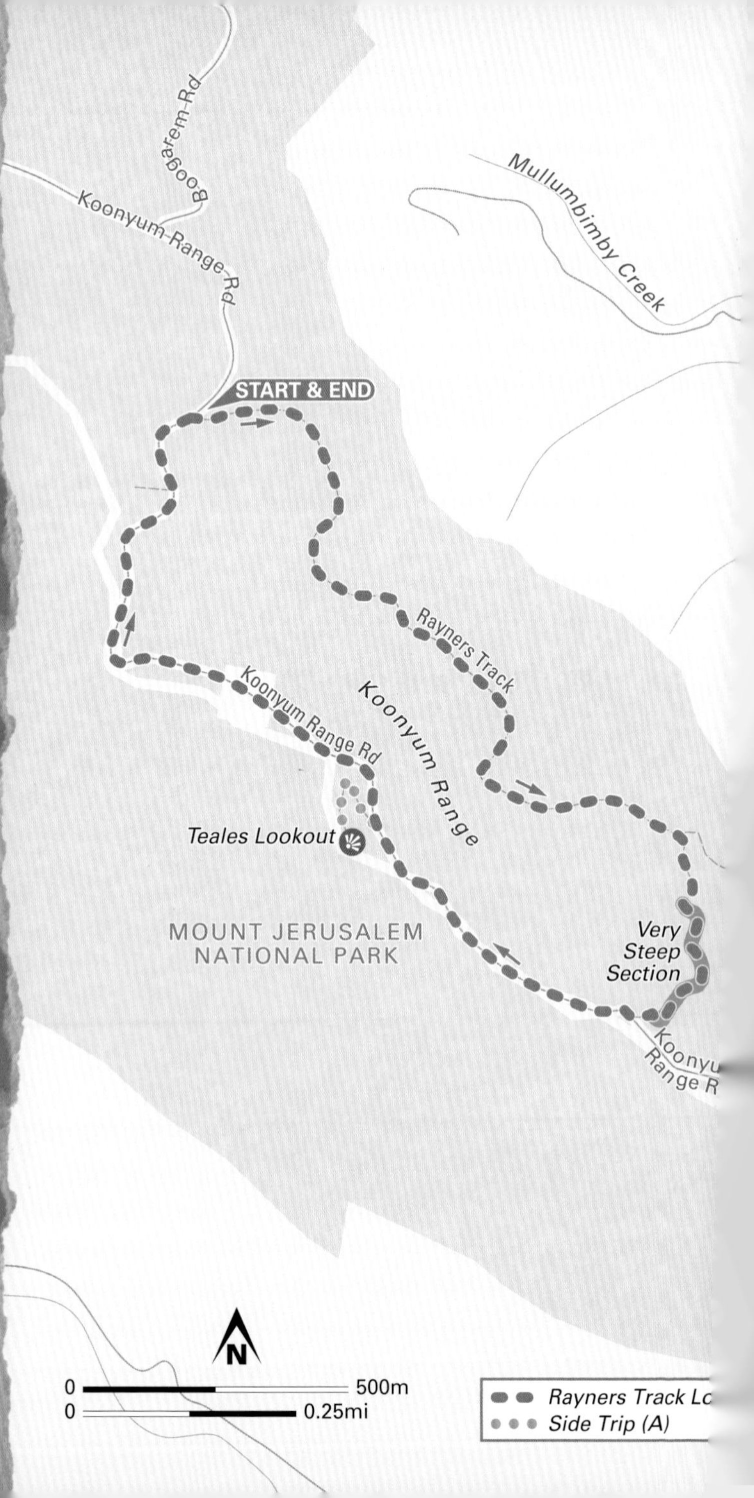
Boogarem Rd
Koonyum Range Rd
Mullumbimby Creek
START & END
Rayners Track
Koonyum Range Rd
Koonyum Range
Teales Lookout
MOUNT JERUSALEM
NATIONAL PARK
Very
Steep
Section
Koonyu
Range R
N
0
500m
0
0.25mi
Rayners Track Lo
Side Trip (A)

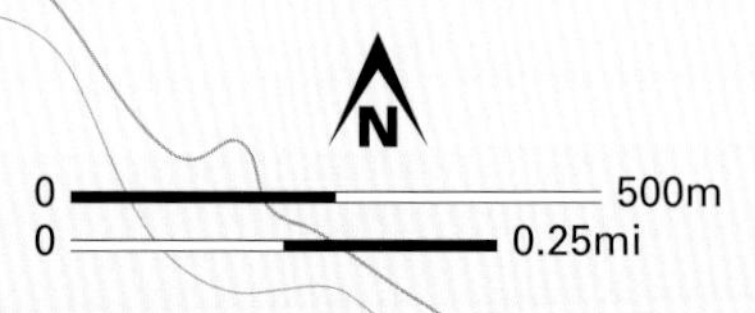

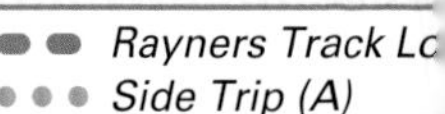

Lake and hinterland views. Good summer walk due to higher altitude and tree shade. Walking shoes needed.

TRAILHEAD: Rayners Track on Koonyum Range Rd

Walk through the gate onto Rayners Track. This fire trail is easy to follow and takes you through pretty forest. After 20 mins you will reach a lake or pond which is a nice place for a rest. The track continues past the lake and suddenly becomes extremely steep for approximately 200m. It then emerges onto Koonyum Range Rd. At the time of writing you needed to walk around orange fencing to get back onto the road. Turn right and walk northwest along Koonyum Range Rd.

SIDE TRIP (A): *After 650m you reach a road to the left that leads up to Teales Lookout. This short side trip rewards you with views across Byron Shire all the way to the coast.*

From the Teales Lookout track proceed along Koonyum Range Rd for 1.8km to return to your starting point.

TERRAIN

Fire trail, one very steep section.

CHALLENGES

Steep slippery section south of the lake. In wet weather consider retracing your steps back from the lake rather than continuing the loop.

GETTING THERE

Rayners Track is 2.1km along Koonyum Range Rd. There is no place to park here so look for a parking space along the roadside before the track.

CAFÉS

Mullumbimby cafés.

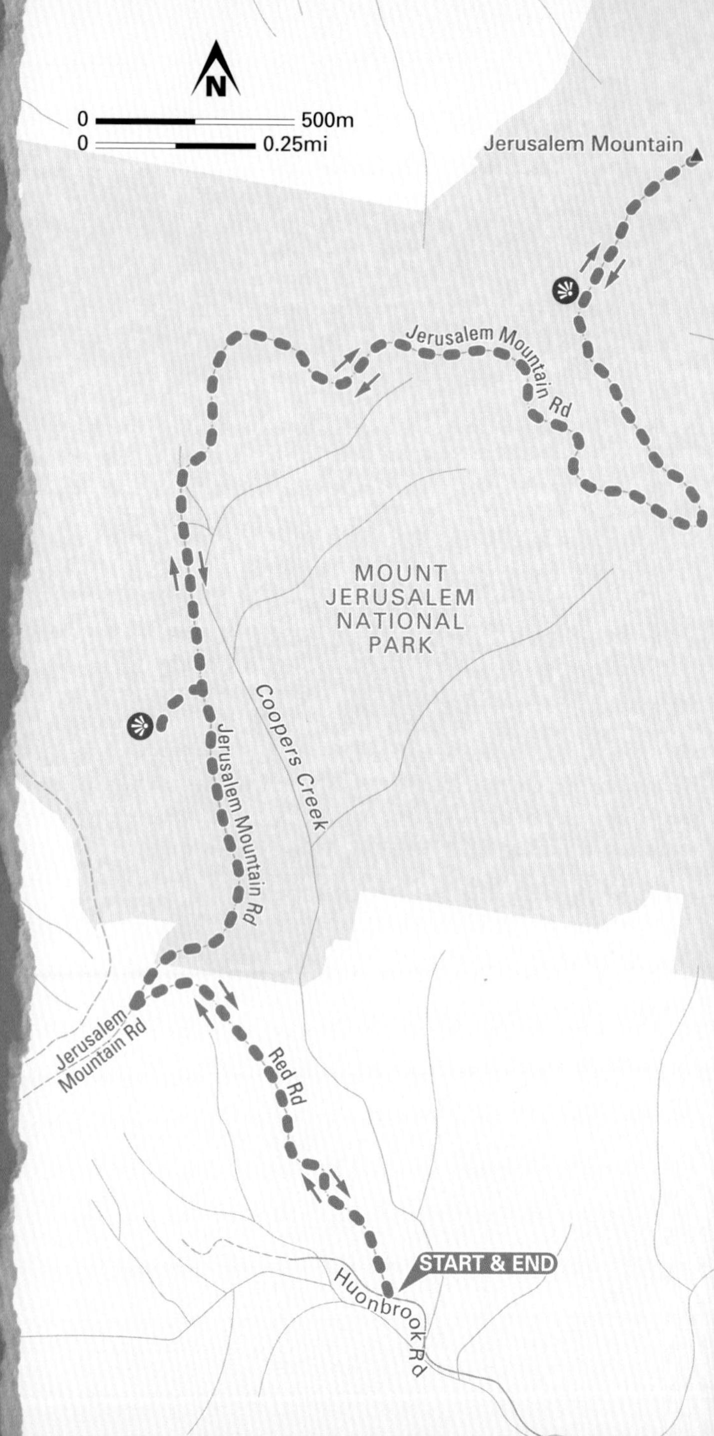

Nearest facilities: Mullumbimby

825m elevation. Challenging climb taking in a hidden knoll with expansive views. Experience and sturdy shoes needed.

NOTE: The first section of this walk is through private land along The Red Rd and the owners graciously allow access. Please respect their property.

TRAILHEAD: Red Rd gate at end of Huonbrook Rd

Close the gate behind you. You are immediately faced with a steep uphill climb. After 350m is a fork; go left through the gate. After a further 650m the track levels out. After another gate there is an immediate sharp turn right onto Jerusalem Mountain Rd which is easy to miss. Take this, pass through another gate and continue to climb, entering Mt Jerusalem National Park.

As the path levels off there is a clearing and an indistinct track leading left to a knoll and sheer cliff. The knoll rewards you with panoramic views to Doughboy Mountain, Wollumbin, Mt Tarrawyra, Mt Matheson and Mt Nardi.

Return to the main track and turn left. The track continues for 1.5km before starting to deteriorate. With some navigation skill, it is still possible to reach the top of Jerusalem Mountain 800m away. At one point the vegetation clears slightly and it looks like you've reached the summit. The clearing to the left here offers further views. The true summit has a directional plaque, but no views.

To return, retrace your steps.

TERRAIN

Fire trail, single track, mostly good surfaces.

CHALLENGES

Navigational challenges, steep terrain and overgrown sections with wait-a-while vine.

Giant stinging tree present in the park (see pg 17).

GETTING THERE

See 'Getting to Huonbrook' on pg 121.

CAFÉS

Mullumbimby cafés.

Tweed Coast

NATURAL ENVIRONMENT

Cabarita coast hosts some of the 25% of original coastal banksia forest that remains on the Tweed coast. What is left is of high conservation value for local fauna as it provides important winter food when many other native plants are not flowering. A small but significant littoral rainforest remnant can be found on Cabarita Hill. This pretty remnant serves as an important ecological link for the coast. Watch out for blue-tongue lizards, brahminy kites, grey goshawks and pied oystercatchers as you walk.

Fingal Head is home to a crescent-shaped mass of hexagonal columns known as the Giant's Causeway. This type of landform occurs in other parts of the world, the most famous being the original Giant's Causeway in County Antrim, Northern Ireland and Fingal's Cave across the water on the isle of Staffa in Scotland. The hexagonal rocks formed when the lava flows from the ancient Tweed Volcano rapidly cooled in the ocean currents. This intriguing rock formation sits just below Fingal Lighthouse on the headland, reaching towards Cook Island.

Along the foredunes are coastal wattle and coastal banksia, while the hind dunes are home to a mixture of eucalypt and rainforest coastal woodland.

Despite its small area, Tweed Heads Historic Site and Ukerebagh Nature Reserve hosts a variety of coastal vegetation. Eucalypt forest and woodland are found near the centre of the site with swamp forest, broad-leaved paperbark and swamp she-oaks thriving in marshy conditions further north. The site has one of the most diverse mangrove communities in NSW, the grey mangrove, producing clusters of small yellow flowers in summer. Originally, there would have been mangroves growing on both sides of the Tweed River for many kilometres. However large amounts of rock were taken from the Fingal Peninsula to create the river walls as well as to reinforce the eastern side of the Tweed River. This exercise was to deepen the main channels for navigation but unfortunately in the process it destroyed large areas of mangroves. The boardwalk track protects what's left of that vegetation on this part of the river. Mangrove communities are some of the harshest environments for life to survive because of the daily movement of tidal waters.

While it can appear in wetter seasons as though the only animal species in existence on the Ukerebagh site are mosquito and midge, you will find others. For butterfly fans there are the blue triangle, black jezebel and endangered blue mangrove butterfly. Shorebirds and waders like the greater egret and royal spoonbill can be seen, particularly at low tide. If you're lucky you might find mangrove kingfishers and honeyeaters.

Tweed Heads West
21 Ukerebagh Walk-on-Water Loop
20 Fingal Head Causeway & Lighthouse
Tweed Heads South
Banora Point
Terranora
Chinderah
Tweed River
Pacific Mwy
Kingscliff
Cudgen
Stotts Creek
Duranbah
SOUTH PACIFIC OCEAN
Casuarina
Cabarita Beach
18 Norries Head Loop
Bogangar
Tanglewood
19 Cabarita Bush Tucker Loop
Round Mountain
Pacific Mwy
Hastings Point
17 Pottsville Eucalyptus Track
N
Pottsville
5km
2mi

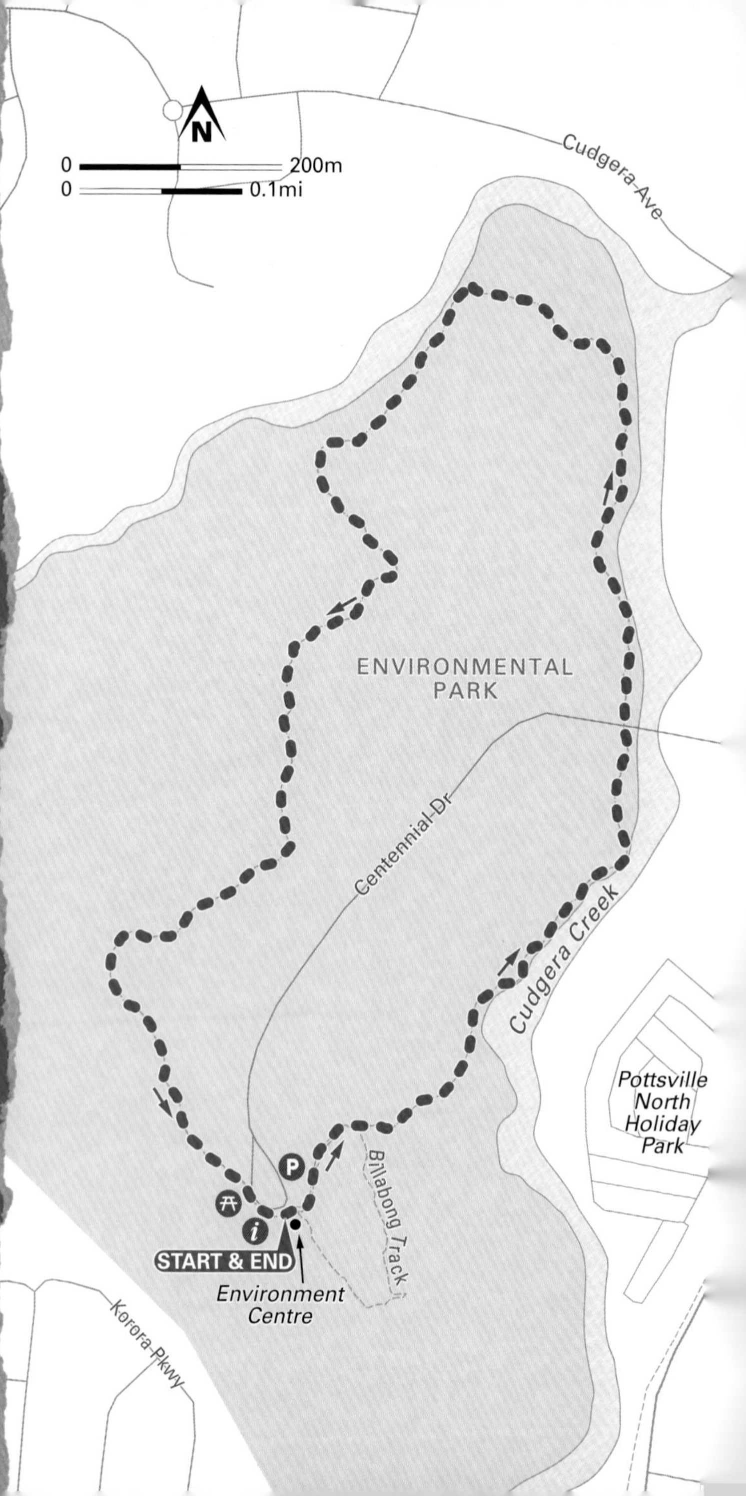

0 200m
0 0.1mi

N

Cudgera Ave

ENVIRONMENTAL PARK

Centennial Dr

Cudgera Creek

Pottsville North Holiday Park

Billabong Track

START & END

Environment Centre

Korora Pkwy

Beautiful creekside forest track through changing landscape with some informational signage. Well signposted.

TRAILHEAD: Pottsville Environment Centre

From the information shelter walk along the path past the Environment Centre to the trail signboard. Follow signs for the Eucalyptus Track. This takes you over a little boardwalk bridge and into the forest. Almost immediately you are greeted with the soothing scent of eucalyptus.

The trail from here is a mixture of forest track and boardwalk and takes you through beautiful forest dominated mainly by paperbark trees. After 300m, Cudgera Creek comes into view. As the trail meanders the creek comes in and out of view and creates a welcome spaciousness in parts.

After 700m, the trail crosses Centennial Dr and continues to skirt the creek. At one point the landscape opens on the right to marshy grassland before reaching the creek edge. This is a nice spot to stop and take in the quiet water view.

From here the track heads south past some big, gnarled, old trees and skirts along the eastern side of the creek before meandering inland through surreal fern forest, paperbark forest and back to the Environment Centre.

TERRAIN

Forest track, boardwalk.

GETTING THERE

Centennial Dr takes you to the Environment Centre in Pottsville Environment Park. Centennial Dr is accessed off Tweed Coast Rd to the north of Pottsville town and runs along the side of Pottsville Sports Club.

CAFÉS

Corner Stop Espresso Bar.

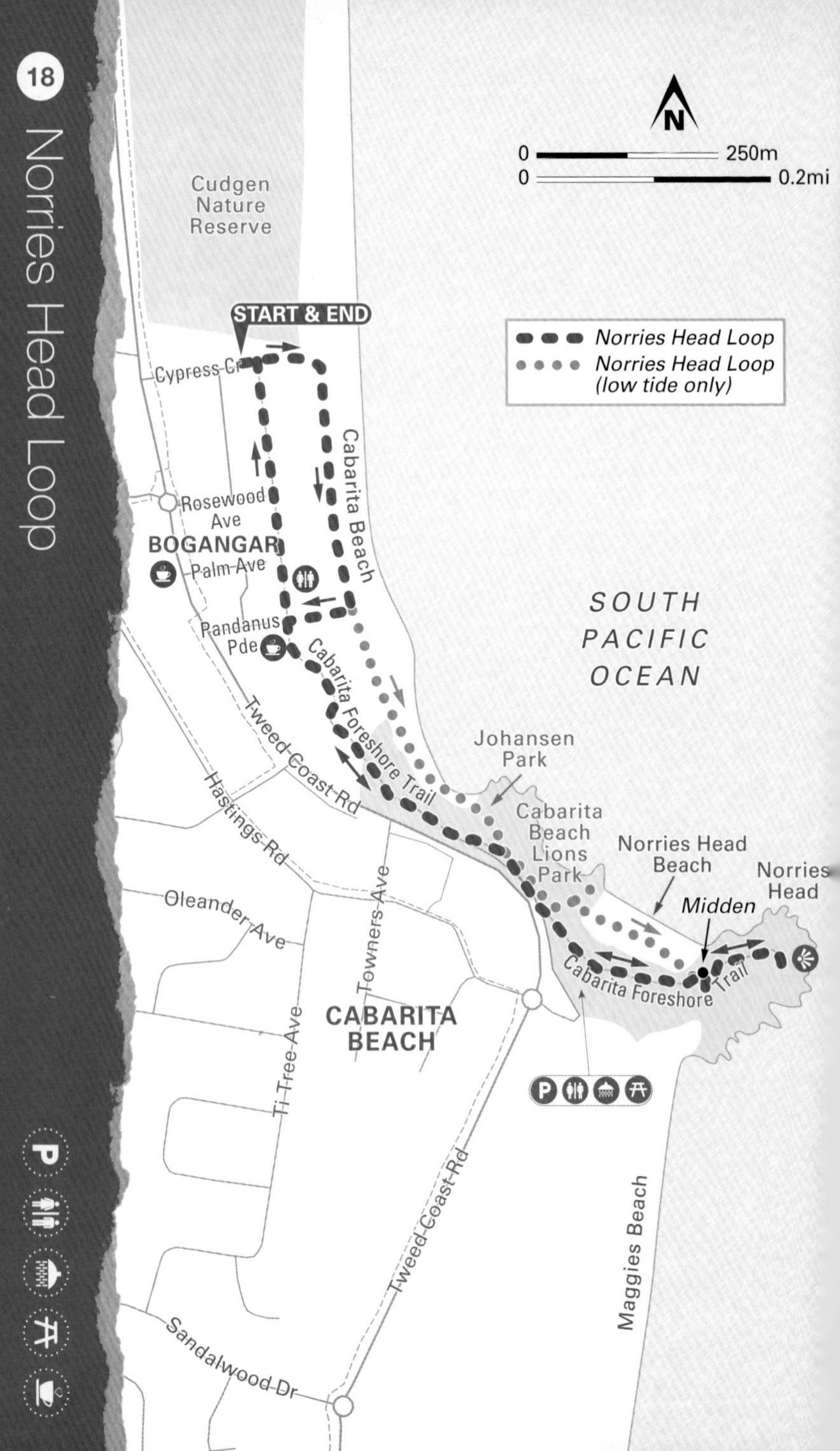
18
Norries Head Loop
N
0
250m
0
0.2mi
Cudgen
Nature
Reserve
START & END
Norries Head Loop
Norries Head Loop
(low tide only)
Cypress Cr
Cabarita Beach
Rosewood
Ave
BOGANGAR
Palm Ave
Pandanus
Pde
Cabarita Foreshore Trail
SOUTH
PACIFIC
OCEAN
Tweed Coast Rd
Hastings Rd
Johansen
Park
Cabarita
Beach
Lions
Park
Norries Head
Beach
Norries
Head
Midden
Oleander Ave
Towners Ave
Cabarita Foreshore Trail
CABARITA
BEACH
Ti-Tree Ave
Tweed Coast Rd
Maggies Beach
Sandalwood Dr

Coastal views north and south from Norries Head. Cabarita Beach rock formations are spectacular.

Note: In high tide the beach sections of this walk will be affected and you may need to keep to the walking tracks. Check byrontrails.com for tides info.

TRAILHEAD: Cypress Cres

From Cypress Cres walk through the dunes to the beach. Turn right and walk south along the beach towards the headland.

After about 10 mins you need to follow boardwalk steps up to Johansen Park above the beach. Turn left and keep to the edge of the fence. After about 100m take the track back down towards the beach. Walk straight out onto the rocky outcrop that separates the beaches before veering right down to the beach. At the end of the beach take the little track up to the boardwalk steps.

From here follow the boardwalk to the Norries Head viewing platform, an ideal place to whale watch in season.

From the viewing platform return along the boardwalk. Once you reach the bottom of the steps continue straight along the sandy track. This takes you past a historical Aboriginal midden site and onwards along the Cabarita Foreshore Trail. Follow the trail along the top of the beach, into the littoral rainforest and along the grassy verge between the beach and the foreshore developments. This takes you back to Cypress Cres.

TERRAIN

Beach, grass, boardwalk and steps.

GETTING THERE

Cypress Cres is off Tweed Coast Rd at the northern end of Cabarita town.

CAFÉS

Coastal Visions Gallery & Café, Marty's at Caba, You & Bamboo.

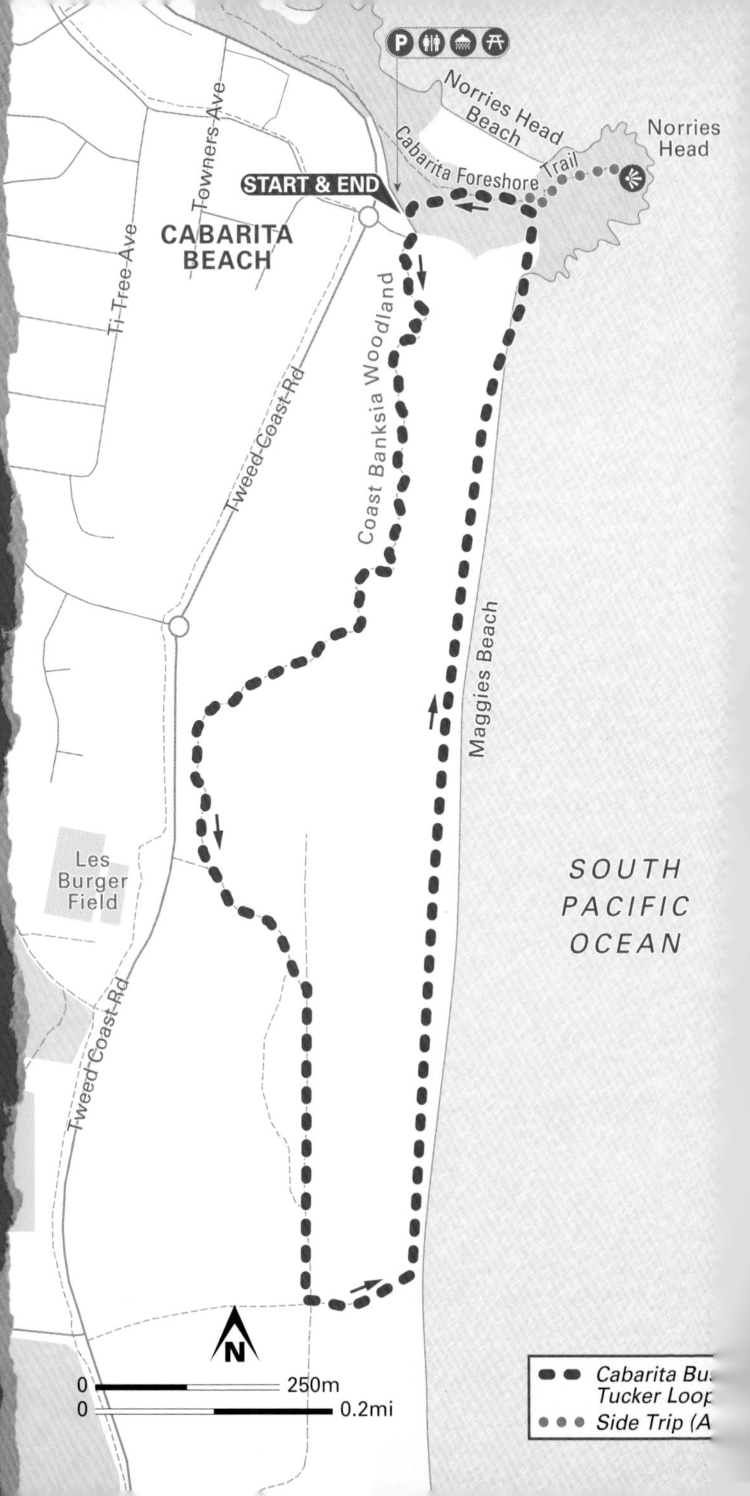

19

Cabarita Bush Tucker Loop

Norries Head Beach
Norries Head
Cabarita Foreshore Trail
START & END
Towners Ave
Ti-Tree Ave
CABARITA BEACH
Tweed Coast Rd
Coast Banksia Woodland
Maggies Beach
Les Burger Field
SOUTH PACIFIC OCEAN
N
0 250m
0 0.2mi

Cabarita Bu[sh] Tucker Loop
Side Trip (A

Signed bush tucker trail takes you through coastal banksia woodland and features screw pinecoastal wattle, sour nuts, beach flax lily, corkwood trees, nasturtium trees, native lasiandra, midgen berry, native guava, pig face, peanut tree, tuckeroo and more.

TRAILHEAD: Cabarita foreshore car park

At the very south end of the car park is a sign for Coast Banksia Woodland and the start of the bush tucker trail. After 100m keep right to stay on the trail. After another 400m the bush tucker trail ends at a junction. Turn right. At the next junction keep left. The trail continues through forest and meanders close to the Tweed Coast Rd before reaching a small gravel road. Turn left and keep right at the next minor junction. You emerge into a clearing with long grasses that swish in the wind, a landscape that is quite a contrast to the previous forest covering. As the track climbs you start to get glimpses and then a view of the ocean. When you reach a four-way junction, turn left for the beach. As you walk north along the beach the beautiful Norries Head looms ever larger. A path at the end of the beach takes you onto the Cabarita Foreshore Trail.

SIDE TRIP (A): ***Take the boardwalk up to Norries Head for some elevation and sea breeze.***

Turn left to complete the loop.

TERRAIN

Bush track and beach.

CHALLENGES

Sun exposure in summer.

GETTING THERE

The Cabarita foreshore car park is off the Tweed Coast Rd at the south end of Cabarita Beach.

CAFÉS

Coastal Visions Gallery & Café, Marty's at Caba, You & Bamboo.

20 Fingal Head Causeway & Lighthouse Walk

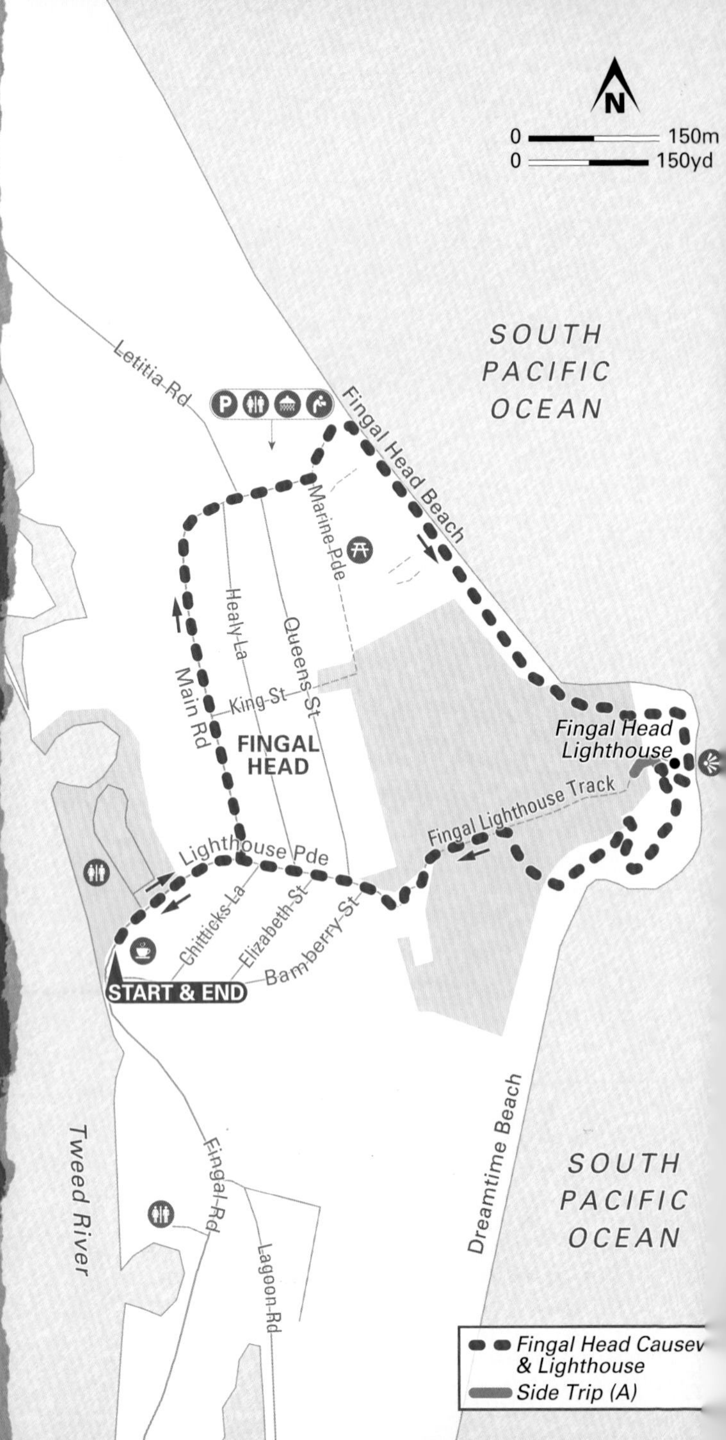

Unique geographical landform set against the backdrop of Cook Island in the near distance. Shoes recommended.

Note: The walk to Fingal Head causeway and lighthouse is only 10 mins. The walk described here takes in more of the area and offers more of a leg stretch.

TRAILHEAD: Sheoak Shack Café

Walk north along Lighthouse Pde. Turn left onto Main Rd and follow the road around to the right towards the ocean, then take the path down onto Fingal Head Beach. Turn right and walk south along the beach. A track leads from the beach up along the headland to the hexagonal columns of the Giant's Causeway (so called after the famous causeway in Northern Ireland). Further on is Fingal Head lighthouse.

SIDE TRIP (A): ***Take a diversion along the boardwalk into the forest to see the foundations of the old lighthouse keeper's cottage.***

From the lighthouse continue south along the headland and descend onto Dreamtime Beach. Here at the northern end of the beach are a few access tracks that will lead you to the Fingal Lighthouse Track. When you reach this formal track turn left. It will take you to Lighthouse Pde. Follow Lighthouse Pde as it veers left towards Tweed River and back to Sheoak Shack Café.

TERRAIN

Grassy verge, beach, boardwalk.

CHALLENGES

Sun exposure in summer.

There are several trail diversions within the headland forest but little chance of getting too lost.

GETTING THERE

Sheoak Shack Café is on Fingal Rd in Fingal Head.

CAFÉS

Sheoak Shack.

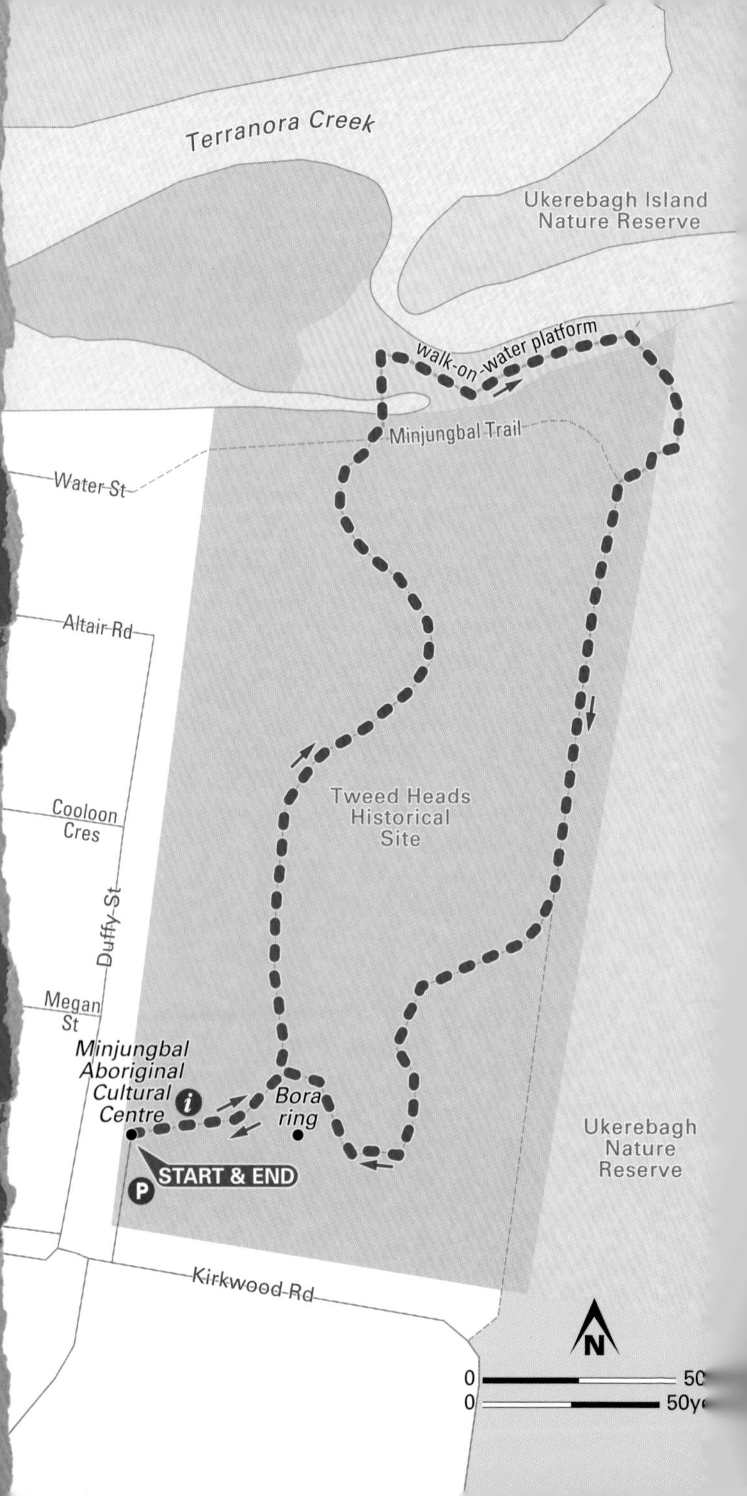

Terranora Creek

Ukerebagh Island Nature Reserve

walk-on-water platform

Minjungbal Trail

Water St

Altair Rd

Cooloon Cres

Duffy St

Megan St

Tweed Heads Historical Site

Minjungbal Aboriginal Cultural Centre

Bora ring

START & END

Ukerebagh Nature Reserve

Kirkwood Rd

N

0 50

0 50y

Best done in the drier seasons as the midges and mozzies make it impossible to enjoy when humid. Minjungbal Aboriginal Cultural Centre provides information on cultural heritage and the site's bora ring.

Note: You can only do this walk during centre hours, 10am – 3pm, Mon–Thurs

TRAILHEAD: Minjungbal Aboriginal Cultural Centre

You may choose to visit the museum and cultural centre first before venturing out onto the track. Guided tours are also offered.

From the car park walk between the museum and cultural centre buildings to find the track. Turn left and follow the track through peaceful eucalypt forest, woodlands and swamp forests. Cross over Minjungbal Trail to the start of the elevated walk-on-water section, which navigates diverse mangrove communities along the Ukerebagh Passage. From here you can also see across the Tweed River to the Ukerebagh Island Nature Reserve, the birthplace of Australia's first Aboriginal senator, Neville Bonner (born 1922), who served in parliament from 1971 to 1983.

The track merges with Minjungbal Trail and then veers right off Minjungbal Trail to take you to the bora ring, one of the main features of this walk. Take some time to imagine the ceremonies that would have been held on this ground. From there the track leads back to the cultural centre.

TERRAIN

Path and boardwalk.

CHALLENGES

Relentless mosquitoes and midges in humid weather.

GETTING THERE

Minjungbal Aboriginal Cultural Centre is on Kirkwood Rd, which is accessed off Minjungbal Dr in South Tweed Heads.

CAFÉS

Sheoak Shack.

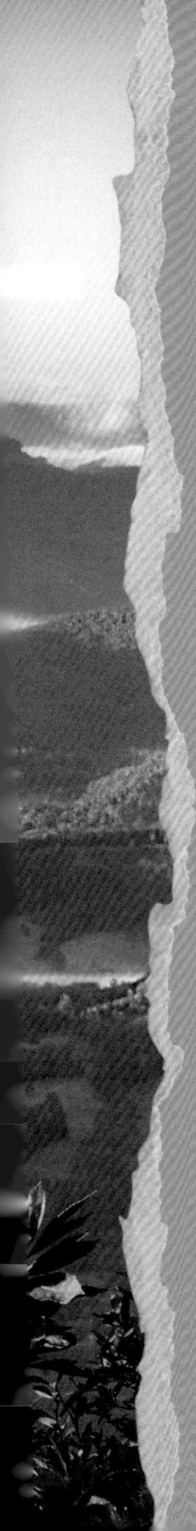

Tweed Hinterland

NATURAL ENVIRONMENT

Mooball National Park is situated along parts of Burringbar and Condong Range on the low eroded eastern sedimentary edge of the Wollumbin caldera. The Burringbar Range consists mostly of phyllitic siltstone and shale along with some quartzites, siliceous sandstones and siltstones and less frequent greywacke and argillite. The range extends all the way to Mt Chowan in the southwest.

Mooball National Park is part of an important habitat corridor for the Tweed region and supports one of the largest lowland moist forest vegetation remnants between the Tweed and Brunswick Valleys. Booyung is plentiful but you will also find bangalow palms and cabbage tree palms in the gullies. Also in the moister areas below the ridgelines you will see blackout, bloodwood and tallowwood. The ridgelines are home to a variety of eucalypts and you will find the occasional brush box or flooded gum.

The park provides important rainforest and lowland habitat for several vulnerable birds and animals. If you keep a keen eye you may spot some fruit doves, owls or marbled frogmouths in the trees, or a long-nosed potoroo, red-legged pademelon, giant barred frog or Stephen's banded snake closer to ground. Other creatures you might come across include the yellow-bellied glider, koalas and a variety of bats as well as the spotted-tailed quoll if you're lucky.

Wollumbin, as mentioned previously, is the remnant

core of the ancient Tweed Volcano. Wollumbin National Park is a Gondwana Rainforest of Australia. You will find a mix of subtropical and warm temperate rainforest on the lower slopes of Wollumbin mountain. Plant species in Wollumbin seem varied to the extreme. There are prettily-named plants such as maidenhair, silkpod, watervine, wait-a-while, tree fern, wilkiea and red apple. These live alongside Wollumbin zieria, with its warty and felted branchlets, the prickly shield fern, stinging nettle, flooded gum, giant spear lily, dogwood, turpentine and, most disconcerting, giant stinging tree. Other plant species include large buttressed carabeens, flame trees, booyongs, strangler figs, Moreton Bay figs, quandong, coachwood, crabapple, Blue Mountain ash, blackbutt, mountain walnut, brush box, flooded gum, mountain wattle, bangalow palm, walking stick palm and shrubby heath.

Many frogs are found in the park, including the pouched frog, the rare and vulnerable hip pocket frog, the great barred frog and the red-eyed tree frog. Low-to-ground fauna include carpet python, land mullet, eastern small-eyed snake, lace monitor, black-bellied marsh snake and long-nosed potoroo. Mammals include red-necked pademelons, swamp wallabies, echidnas, spotted-tailed quolls, brushtail possums, ringtail possums, gliders, koalas and bats.

The rich diversity of the rainforest attracts a whole range of birds; more common varieties include catbirds, rifle birds, regent and satin bower birds, rosellas, parrots, finches, mistletoe birds, various fruit-eating pigeons, treecreepers, robins and wrens, as well as the sooty owl, monarch flycatcher and the crested hawk. Some rare species to be found are the Albert's lyrebird, rufous scrub-bird, marbled frogmouth and wompoo fruit-pigeon.

Tyalgum Creek

Mebbi Nation Park

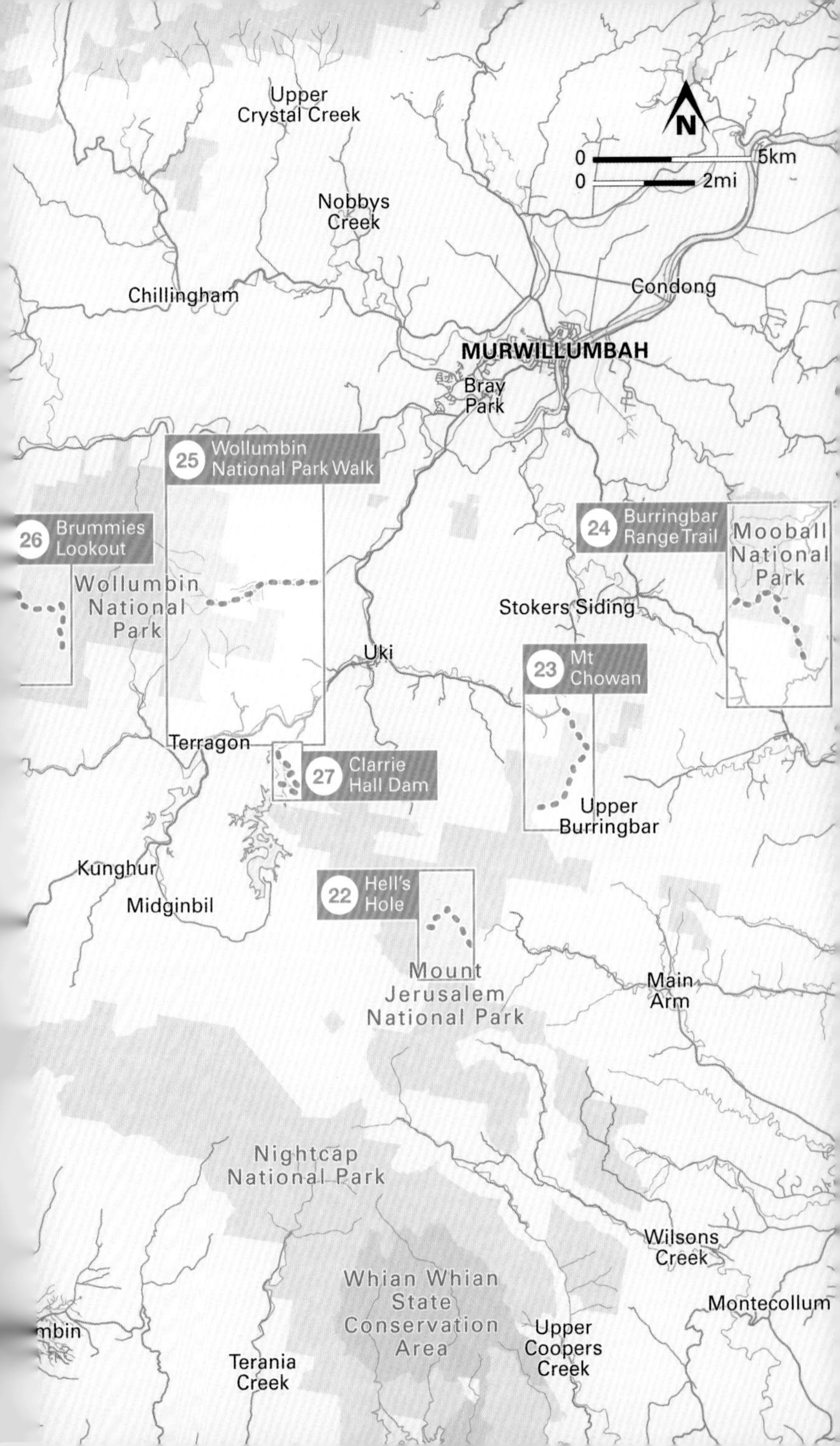
Upper
Crystal Creek
0
5km
0
2mi
Nobbys
Creek
Chillingham
Condong
MURWILLUMBAH
Bray
Park
25 Wollumbin
National Park Walk
26 Brummies
Lookout
24 Burringbar
Range Trail
Mooball
National
Park
Wollumbin
National
Park
Stokers Siding
Uki
23 Mt
Chowan
Terragon
27 Clarrie
Hall Dam
Upper
Burringbar
Kunghur
Midginbil
22 Hell's
Hole
Mount
Jerusalem
National Park
Main
Arm
Nightcap
National Park
Wilsons
Creek
Whian Whian
State
Conservation
Area
Montecollum
Upper
Coopers
Creek
Terania
Creek

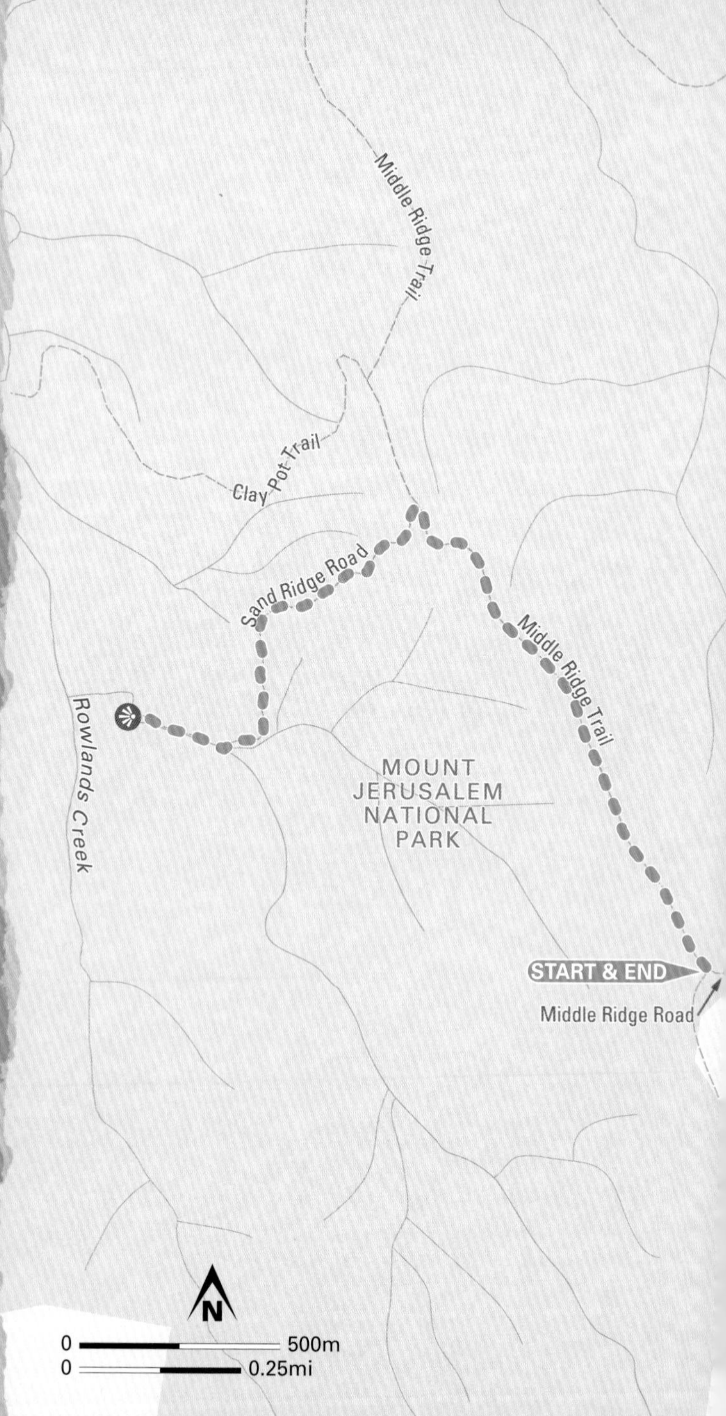

Nearest facilities: Uki and Main Arm

Picturesque creekscape. Pretty forest track. Walking shoes recommended.

TRAILHEAD: Gate on Middle Ridge Trail

Middle Ridge Trail makes an easy descent for 1.4km through pretty forest before reaching a clearing, marked by a large, old, hollowed tree stump. There are three track options at this point – two small single tracks and the continuation of the main track. Take the second single track to the right of the tree stump (Sand Ridge Rd).

Half a kilometre along this track a view to the hills in the northwest opens up. After this the track veers south and starts to descend more steadily into a beautiful gullied forest area. Along here you'll see the remnant stumps of some mighty old trees that have long since been cut down as well as some large fallen trees which you may need to navigate around. At the bottom of the road is a creek and a very old wooden bridge. As you cross beware the holes in the bridge hidden by overgrown grass. Immediately after the bridge veer right and walk along the side of the creek to the pools for a dip.

To return, retrace your steps upstream to Sand Ridge Rd. Turn left, cross the bridge and climb uphill to the large clearing and junction. Turn right onto Middle Ridge Trail to return to the gate and your starting point.

TERRAIN

Fire trail, single track, uneven ground.

CHALLENGES

Hidden holes in the wooden bridge at the bottom of Sand Ridge Rd.

Consider not using repellent or sunscreen if you plan to swim.

GETTING THERE

Inside Mt Jerusalem National Park take the turn off Main Arm Rd for Middle Ridge Rd. After 1.2km is a fork, a gate and a sign for Middle Ridge Trail. Park here.

CAFÉS

Main Arm General Store, Uki Café & Art Gallery.

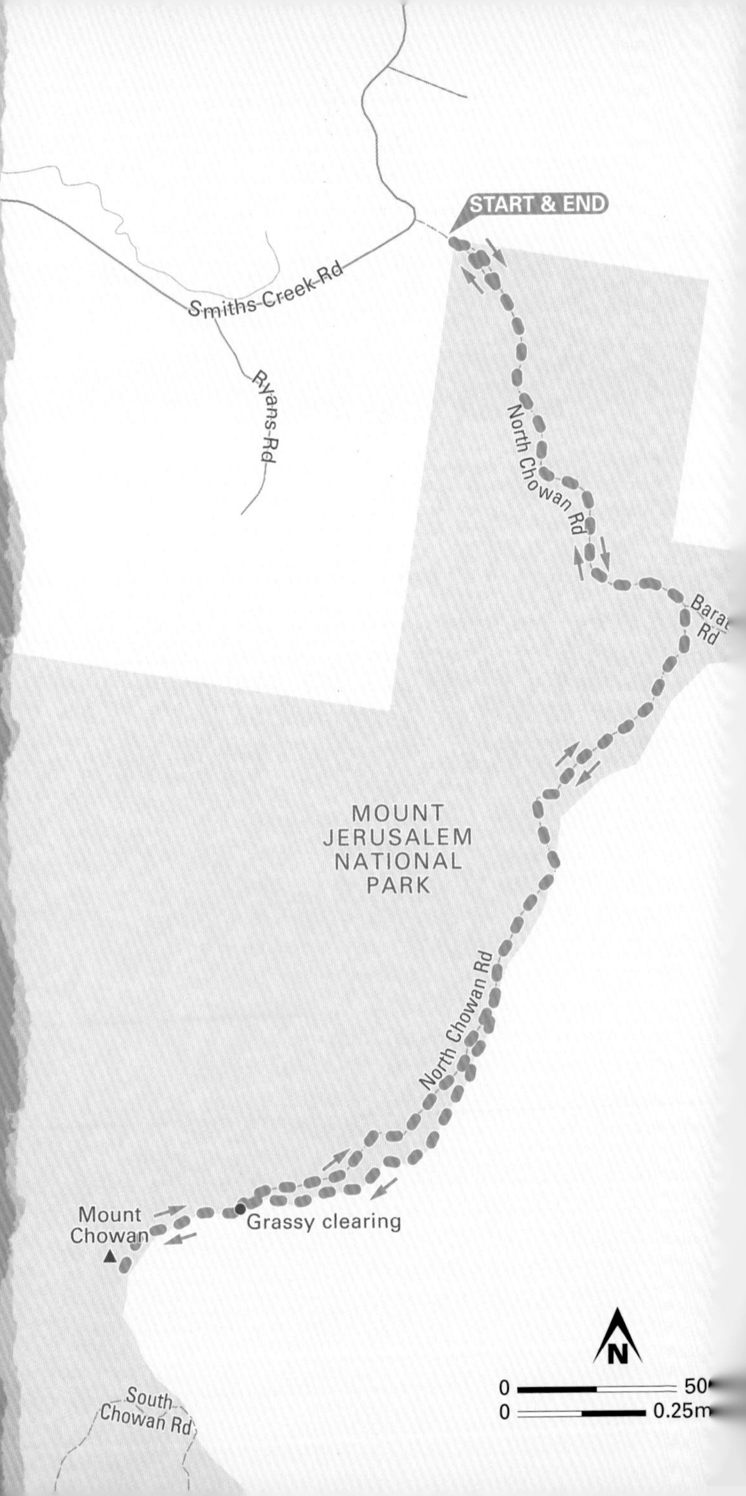

START & END
Smiths Creek Rd
Ryans Rd
North Chowan Rd
Barat Rd
MOUNT JERUSALEM NATIONAL PARK
North Chowan Rd
Mount Chowan
Grassy clearing
South Chowan Rd
N
0 50
0 0.25m

Nearest facilities: Uki

500m elevation. Can be done as a loop of sorts as there are two tracks that run parallel to each other. Sturdy walking shoes needed.

TRAILHEAD: Gate on North Chowan Rd

As soon as you walk through the gate into the national park you are greeted by a fork, with the fire trail to your right and the single track to your left. The fire trail is barren but has great views on the ascent; the single track offers a more interesting forest experience. Take the left to begin. This single track rejoins the fire trail after 5 to 10 minutes and then breaks off to the left again. This continues to happen for the length of the fire trail (4km). Take the fire trail for the next two sections to catch the views of Mt Chowan. Ignore the left turn for Baratta Rd. You may want to take the single track for the next section of parallel track.

At the last point of convergence is a grassy clearing, a nice spot for a break before launching into the steep ascent of Mt Chowan. A single track takes you up, with expansive and beautiful views, extending to Wollumbin in the northwest. The track curves around the mountain, about 8m below the top, and eventually starts to descend along the southern track. If you attempt to find the summit be aware of how to get back to the track.

To return, retrace your steps to the grassy clearing and continue the descent along either track. Both will take you back to your starting point.

TERRAIN

Fire trail, single track; some steep sections.

CHALLENGES

Loose rocks and overgrown vegetation along the summit section.

GETTING THERE

Access North Chowan Rd from Smith's Creek Rd (between Stokers Siding and Uki). 4km after Stokers Siding take the unsigned road to the left at the hairpin bend Drive to the gate and park.

CAFÉS

Uki Café & Art Gallery.

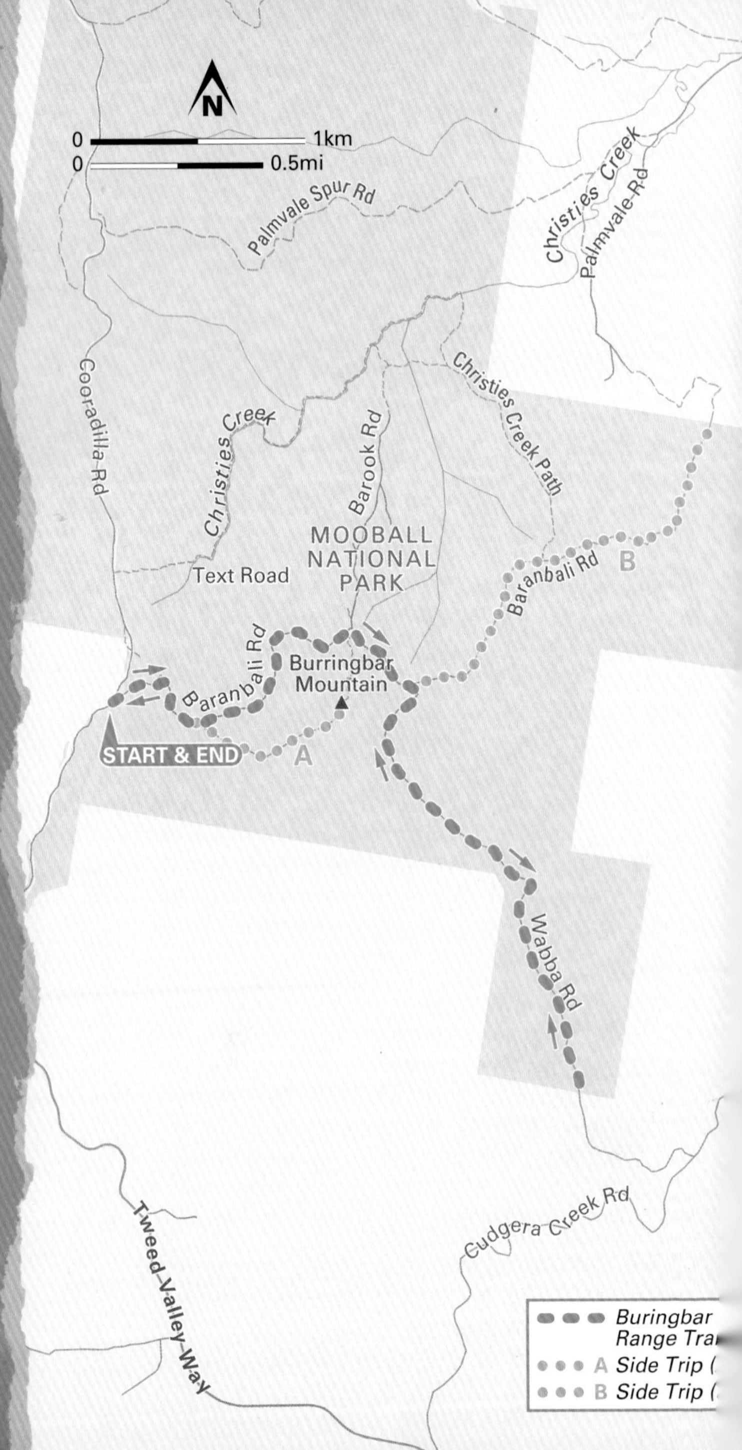

Burringbar village has the closest facilities.

Shaded summer walk in Mooball National Park. Partial views to Springbrook Plateau, the Cougals and the coast. Some pretty palm-filled gullies, grass trees, flooded gums and red cedar. Walking shoes needed.

TRAILHEAD: Junction of Cooradilla Rd and Baranbali Rd

From the gate begin the walk along Baranbali Rd. Keep left at the first fork to stay on Baranbali Rd.

SIDE TRIP (A): ***The right fork takes you along overgrown single track to the top of Mt Burringbar (391m). You need to bush bash to get there.***

The road swings left and offers views of Springbrook and the twin peaks of the Cougals. When you reach the T-junction turn right. At the next Y take a right and walk along Wabba Rd. There are views through the trees to the coast along this section. This track eventually takes you to the southeastern boundary of the park.

To return, retrace your steps, taking a left onto Baranbali Rd and walking back to the gate.

SIDE TRIP (B): ***Turn right onto Baranbali Rd and walk to the eastern boundary of the park (2.2km each way). This track also offers some coastal views.***

TERRAIN

Fire trail.

CHALLENGES

Leeches after rain.

Possible long grass.

GETTING THERE

Cooradilla Rd is unsigned and accessed off Tweed Valley Way between Burringbar and Murwillumbah. Driving from the south watch out for a picnic shelter on a right-hand curve, 4km after Burringbar. Cooradilla Rd is on your right.

CAFÉS

Tweed Gallery Café, Moo Moo Roadhouse, Burringbar General Store.

N
0 1km
0 0.5mi

WOLLUMBIN
NATIONAL
PARK

Korrumbyn Creek
Mt Warning Rd
START & END
Lyrebird
Lookout
Mount
Warning
Mount Uki
The Sisters
Tweed River
Kyogle Rd

P

Slow, steady climb through beautiful countryside into subtropical rainforest. Walking shoes needed.

TRAILHEAD: Korrumbyn Creek roadside area

Korrumbyn Creek is shaded and very accessible from this spot and makes for a peaceful orientation to the Wollumbin area. It can be nice to sit by the creekside before beginning your walk.

Walk west along Mt Warning Rd which crosses Korrumbyn Creek, swings to the right and climbs steadily uphill. There are beautiful views into the creek valley at several places along the road. At one point the road gets quite narrow so walk with care. The last kilometre into Wollumbin National Park is quite steep. You pass a toilet block on your left and car parking on your right. When you reach the end of the road you are rewarded with cool, shady rainforest trees and the Breakfast Creek picnic area.

A stony path leads to the right and takes you over Breakfast Creek to Lyrebird Lookout, a short 150m walk.

Return the way you came along Mt Warning Rd. The descent will be faster than the ascent and should take less time.

TERRAIN

Road.

CHALLENGES

Cars on the road.

GETTING THERE

Korrumbyn Creek roadside area is 2.3km along Mt Warning Rd.

CAFÉS

Mavis's Kitchen, Rainforest Café, Uki Café & Art Gallery.

26

Brummies Lookout

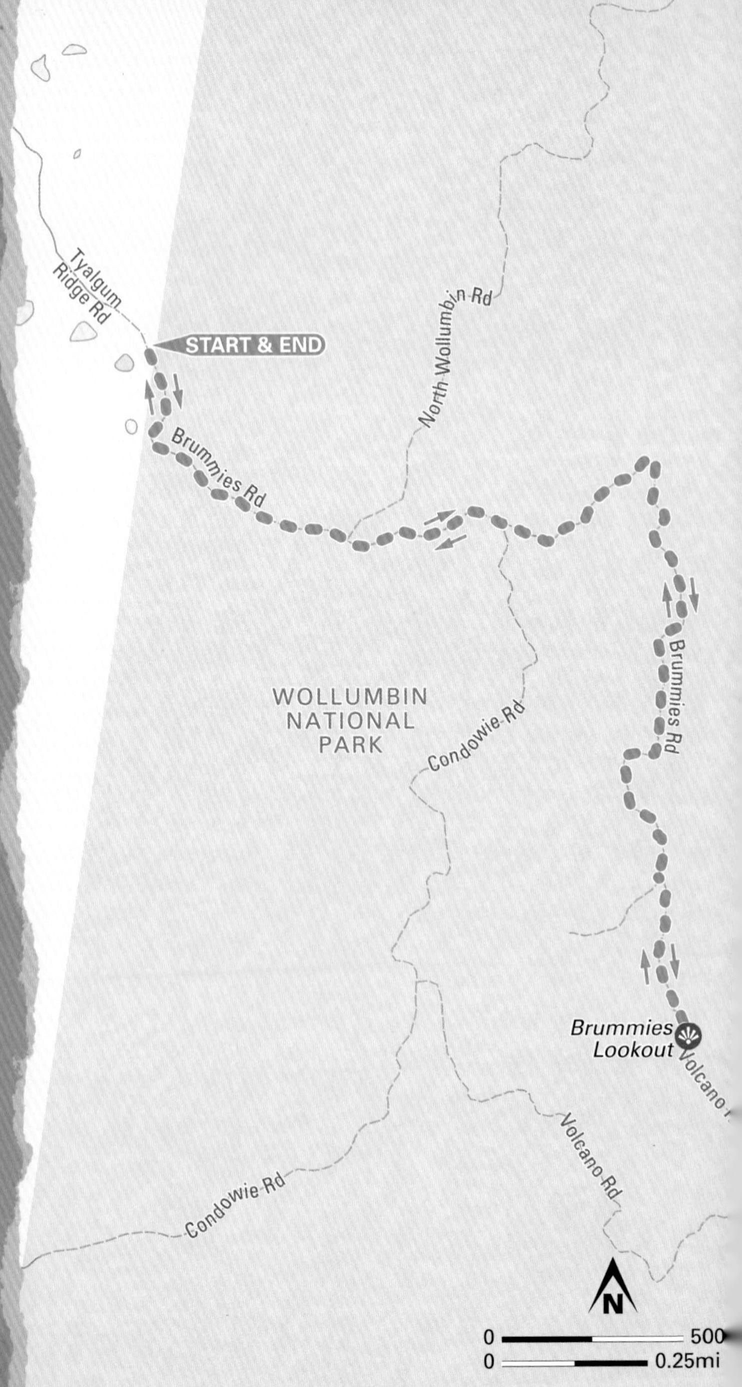

Nearest facilities: Tyalgum

Vast and rare views of the sheer western cliff face of Wollumbin. Panoramas to the Border Ranges. Experience needed for the final ascent and descent. Sturdy walking shoes needed.

TRAILHEAD: Gate on Brummies Rd

20 mins after the gate the road forks at North Wollumbin Rd. Continue straight on Brummies Rd. After another 10 mins keep left at the next fork (for Condowie Rd). Continue the steady climb along Brummies Rd for another 2km.

As the trail starts getting overgrown watch out for old, unmaintained stone steps on the left (easy to miss). If you reach the end of Brummies Rd you have gone too far.

Take the steps and climb up a semi-worn and unmaintained path through magnificent grass trees to Brummies Lookout. You will be rewarded with spectacular views of Wollumbin, the Border Ranges and even some glimpses of Lamington Plateau. You can continue to the top of the peak but the best views are where the forest opens up about two-thirds of the way to the top.

Finding the path back down from the lookout is trickier so be alert. If you do lose the path, stop, retrace your steps uphill to the last place where the route was clear and look for the most obvious track. This will take you back to Brummies Rd.

Once on Brummies Rd turn right and retrace your steps back to the gate.

TERRAIN

Fire trail, rocky terrain, unmaintained track.

CHALLENGES

Unmarked, unmaintained, steep track.

GETTING THERE

Just before Tyalgum take Swift's Rd off Tyalgum Rd. Follow the sign for Wollumbin National Park. This takes you to a gate where you can park. The end of the road is extremely worn.

CAFÉS

Flutterbies Cottage Café.

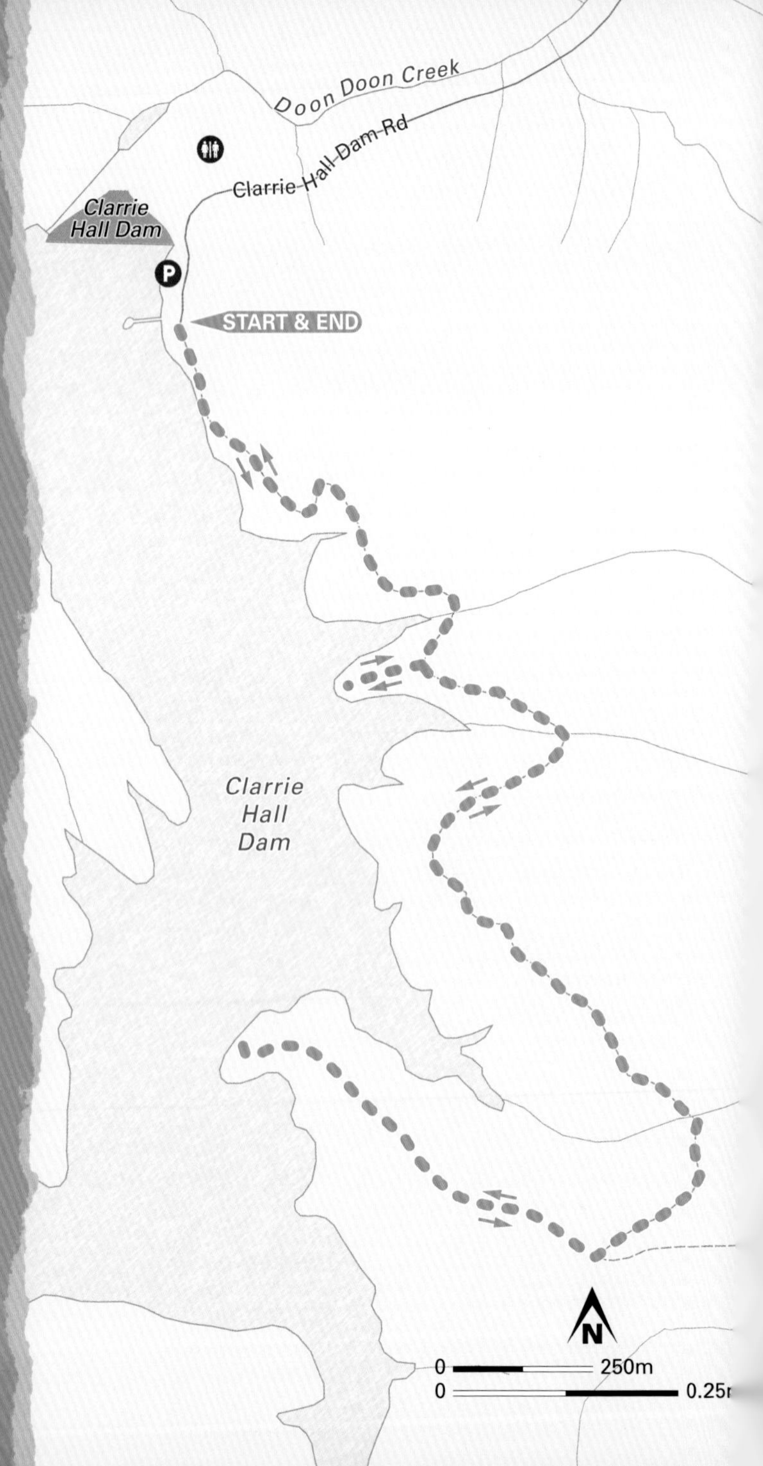

Doon Doon Creek
Clarrie Hall Dam Rd
Clarrie Hall Dam Rd
Clarrie Hall Dam
P
START & END
Clarrie Hall Dam
N
0
250m
0
0.25

Water views south and west across the dam. Walking shoes needed.

TRAILHEAD: Boat ramp at Clarrie Hall Dam wall

From the boat ramp follow the trail that meanders south along the eastern edge of the water. Keep to the right, ignoring forks that lead off to other trails on the left. Take the first trail fork to your right which leads to the water's edge and some views across the dam.

Make the short return to the main trail and turn right. After 1.2km is a signpost saying 'Dam Wall Trail'. Turn right and walk downhill, again to the water's edge. To the east across the dam is the unfortunately named Mt Misery.

Return uphill to the main trail. Turn left and walk back to the boat ramp the way you came.

TERRAIN

Fire trail.

GETTING THERE

Clarrie Hall Dam Rd is 3.3km south west of Uki. The road comes to an end at the dam.

CAFÉS

Uki Café & Art Gallery.

North Ballina Coast

NATURAL ENVIRONMENT

Lennox headland consists of shallow krasnozem soils overlying the Lismore Basalts (formed by lava from the volcano's earliest eruptions). South of the headland basalt boulders blanket the beach to which they lend their name, Boulder Beach. Further south again is Rocky Point, a stunning headland again formed from the movement of basalt lava over coal sediment. One of the most significant features along this coastline is Flat Rock, a prominent rock platform that is claimed to be the most easterly point in Australia at low tide. The rocky shoreline is an important intertidal habitat for marine life. The greater platform, beach and dune area is a resting and roosting habitat for several regional and migratory seabirds as well as sea turtles.

High up on Lennox headland you will find a number of tiny rainforest remnants. Remnant littoral rainforest can be found on the southern end of Boulder Beach (an area of high conservation value) and along Angels Beach. There are also some infrequent littoral rainforest trees behind the dunes of Sharps Beach and Shelly Beach. The southern side of Rocky Point headland is home to a dense cottonwood colony, one of the few remaining on the Ballina coast. Kangaroo grass grows on the northern and southern areas of Skennars Head and some small and rare herbs grow among the grasses of the headland as well as prolific paper daisies. Coastal banksias are abundant on the northern side of Skennars Head and taper off as you go south, appearing again along Sharps Beach.

This coastline is home to several threatened birds. If lucky you might see an osprey hunting offshore. Other birds seen in the area include the jabiru, the sooty oystercatcher, the pied oystercatcher, the beach stone-curlew and the black-winged petrel. The black flying fox or grey-headed flying fox are important creatures for this area as they disperse fruit seeds and pollinate native flowers.

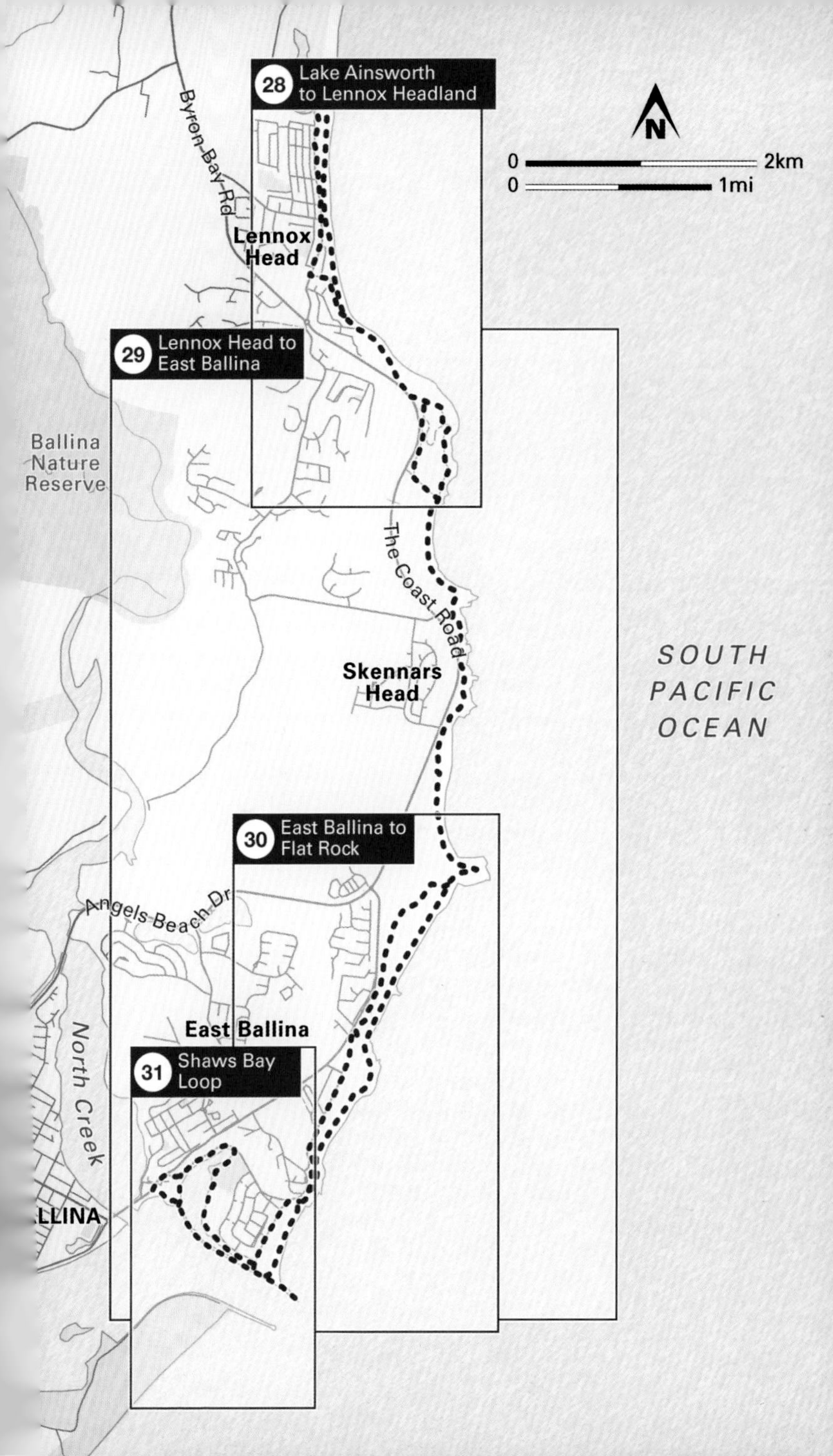
28
Lake Ainsworth to Lennox Headland
0
2km
0
1mi
N
Byron Bay Rd
Lennox Head
29
Lennox Head to East Ballina
Ballina Nature Reserve
The Coast Road
Skennars Head
SOUTH PACIFIC OCEAN
30
East Ballina to Flat Rock
Angels Beach Dr
East Ballina
31
Shaws Bay Loop
North Creek
LLINA

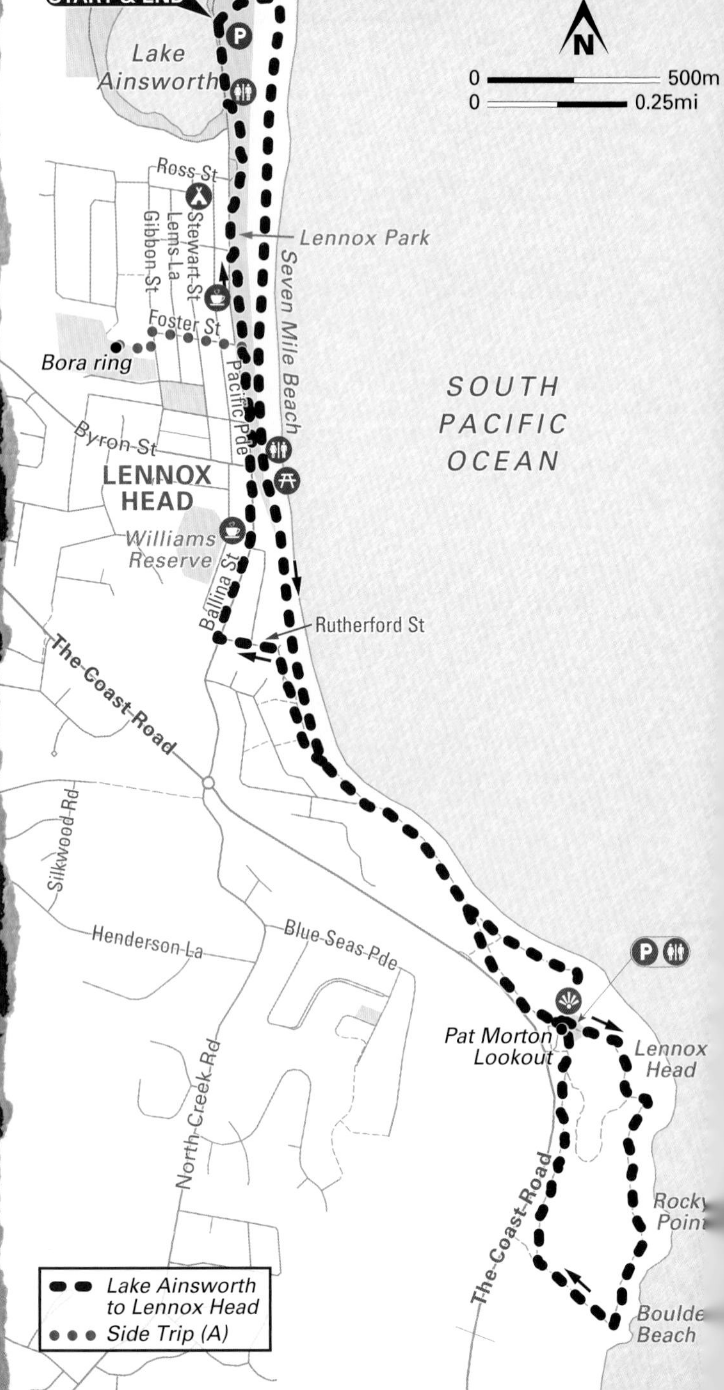
START & END
Lake Ainsworth
0 500m
0 0.25mi
N
Ross St
Stewart St
Lems La
Gibbon St
Lennox Park
Seven Mile Beach
Foster St
Bora ring
Pacific Pde
SOUTH PACIFIC OCEAN
Byron St
LENNOX HEAD
Williams Reserve
Ballina St
Rutherford St
The Coast Road
Silkwood Rd
Henderson La
Blue Seas Pde
North Creek Rd
Pat Morton Lookout
Lennox Head
Rocky Point
Boulder Beach
Lake Ainsworth to Lennox Head
Side Trip (A)

The calmness of the tea tree lake contrasts with the vigour of the headland exposure. Stunning coastal views. Great whale-watching vantage point.

TRAILHEAD: Turning circle on Pacific Pde

From Lake Ainsworth take a track to Seven Mile Beach. Walk south to the end of the beach and pick up the path to Pat Morton Lookout. After 600m the path forks. Take the left fork and follow this smaller trail along the edge of the shore to a small clearing marked by a bench and a four-way junction. Take one of the tracks uphill to the car park. Continue up the steps to the lookout. From the lookout the track carries on along the cliff edge downhill towards Skennars Head.

Walk down to the edge of Boulder Beach then turn right. The track takes you towards the road, swings uphill parallel to the road and takes you back to the Pat Morton Lookout car park.

Head back to town along the main pathway. The pathway merges onto Rutherford St and takes you to Ballina St where you turn right. Some 400m along Ballina St is Lennox Park. From here there is a meandering path along grassy verge that takes you back to Lake Ainsworth. One short section goes along the road.

SIDE TRIP (A): *To visit the bora ring on Gibbon St, turn left from Pacific Pde onto Foster St, then a left onto Gibbon St. The entrance is across the road.*

TERRAIN

Paved path, beach, single track.

CHALLENGES

Sun exposure in summer.

Track on the southern side of the headland can be slippery when wet.

GETTING THERE

Lake Ainsworth is well signposted from Lennox Head town. About 350m after the intersection between Pacific Pde and Camp Drewe Rd is a turning circle and shaded parking area.

CAFÉS

Lennox Heads cafés.

29 Lennox Head to East Ballina

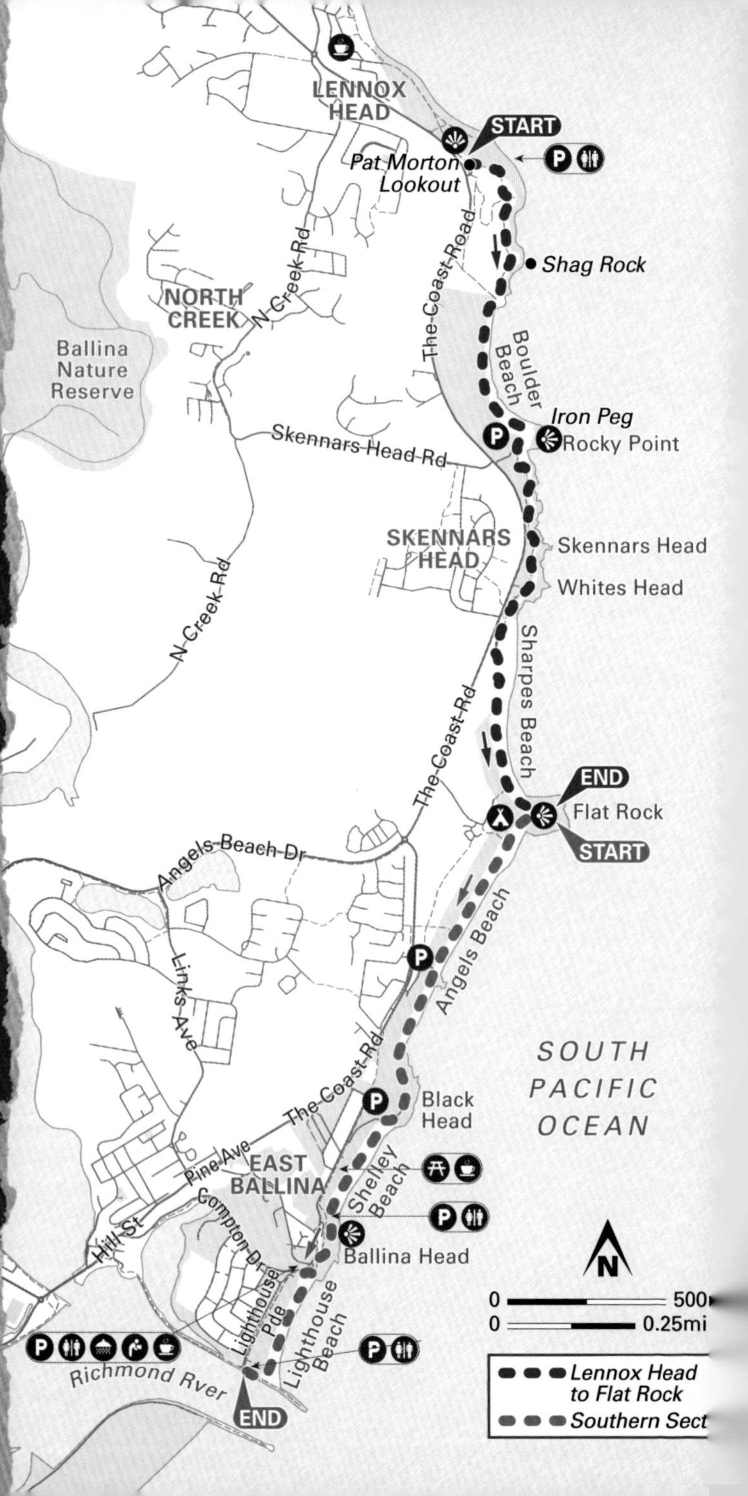
LENNOX HEAD
START
Pat Morton Lookout
Shag Rock
NORTH CREEK
N Creek Rd
The Coast Road
Ballina Nature Reserve
Boulder Beach
Iron Peg
Rocky Point
Skennars Head Rd
SKENNARS HEAD
Skennars Head
Whites Head
Sharpes Beach
N Creek Rd
The Coast Rd
END
Flat Rock
START
Angels Beach Dr
Angels Beach
Links Ave
SOUTH PACIFIC OCEAN
The Coast Rd
Black Head
Pine Ave
EAST BALLINA
Shelley Beach
Compton Dr
Hill St
Ballina Head
Lighthouse Pde
Lighthouse Beach
Richmond Rver
END
N
0
500
0
0.25mi
Lennox Head to Flat Rock
Southern Sect

Breathtaking Ballina coastline. Walking shoes needed.

NOTE: Two-part walk – you can do one section return, or if you have a group drop cars at each end and walk one way.

TRAILHEAD: Pat Morton Lookout

NORTHERN SECTION (5.1KM ONE WAY, 2 HRS): From the car park take the steps from the lookout and continue along the cliff edge, downhill past Shag Rock towards Boulder Beach. Walk to the southern end of the beach, then take the track that leads up to a spectacular grassy headland and Rocky Point. The headland gives way to a smaller beach alcove; walk along the top of it and pick up the grassy track that leads through beautiful littoral rainforest over the top of spectacular Skennars Head and continues along the clifftop to Whites Head. The track eventually reaches Sharpes Beach car park. From here walk down onto the beach and continue south to Flat Rock, a large protruding rocky platform.

SOUTHERN SECTION (3.7KM ONE WAY, 1 HR): Continue walking south from Flat Rock along Angels Beach. When the beach ends pick your way through rocky sand to reach Black Head. Continue around the head to Shelly Beach. At the far end of the beach a paved path takes you around Ballina Head to Lighthouse Beach. Walk to the southern end of Lighthouse Beach and climb up to the North Wall. Turn right along the wall and you will reach the marine rescue tower.

TERRAIN

Beach, single track, uneven ground.

CHALLENGES

Sun exposure in summer.

GETTING THERE

Pat Morton Lookout and car park is south of Lennox Head town and is well signposted.

CAFÉS

Lighthouse Beach Café, The Belle General, Lennox Heads cafés.

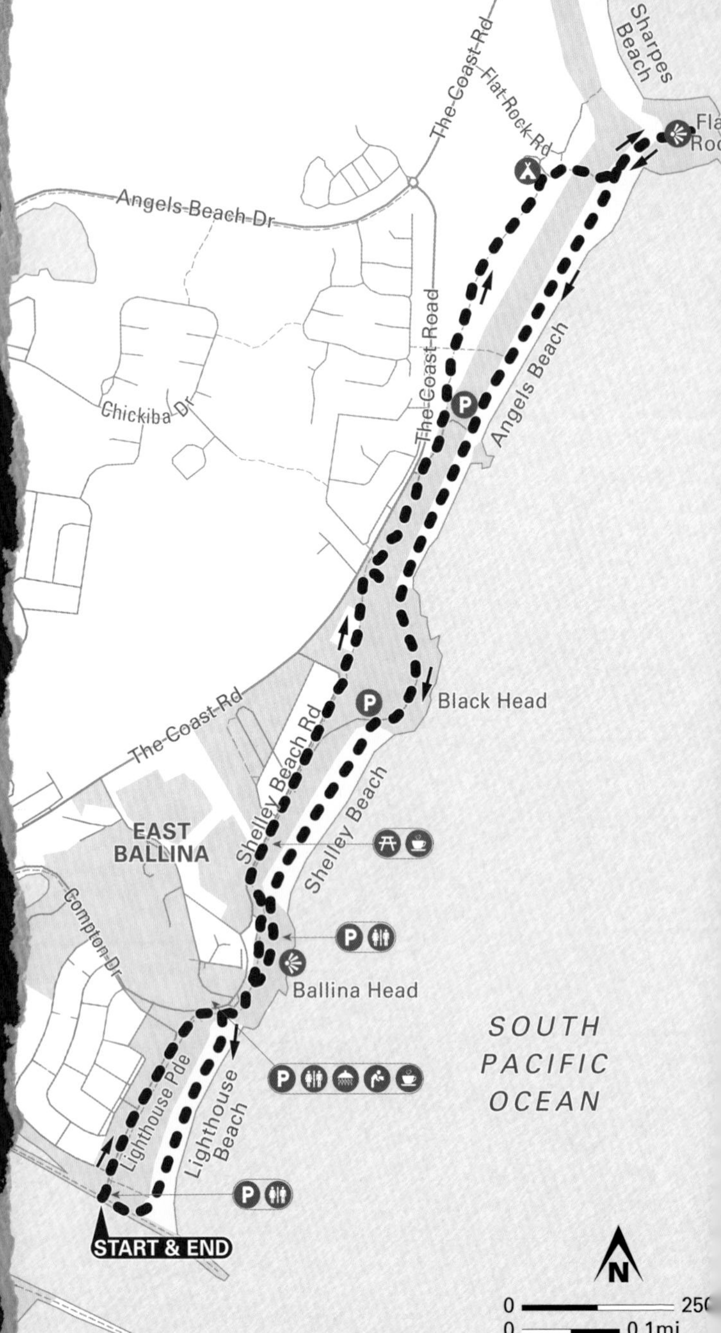

Sharpes Beach
Flat Rock
Flat Rock Rd
The Coast Rd
Angels Beach Dr
The Coast Road
Angels Beach
Chickiba Dr
Black Head
The Coast Rd
Shelley Beach Rd
Shelley Beach
EAST BALLINA
Compton Dr
Ballina Head
SOUTH PACIFIC OCEAN
Lighthouse Pde
Lighthouse Beach
START & END
N
0
0
0.1mi

Takes in the Ballina coast from Richmond River to Flat Rock (the most easterly point in Australia at low tide). Coastal rainforest and rugged coast.

TRAILHEAD: Marine rescue tower on Lighthouse Pde

Walk north along Lighthouse Pde, picking up the coastal path beside Ballina Lighthouse and Lismore SLSC to Ballina Head and Shelly Beach Rd. Where Shelly Beach Rd swings sharply left, follow the footpath veering right into littoral rainforest and East Ballina Aboriginal Place.

After 10 mins (400m) is a track to the right with an overhead Heritage Walk sign (the second such sign). Take this track. After only 30m is a junction. Turn left. Continue straight through the four-way junction and the car parking area. Where the sealed road ends two walking tracks diverge; take the left. Continue straight at the next four-way junction. The track emerges at Flat Rock Tent Park. Keep the tree line to your right to find the track to the beach and Flat Rock.

To return, walk south from Flat Rock along Angels Beach to rocky Black Head. Continue around the head to Shelly Beach and walk to the end of the beach to reach the paved path you took earlier. Walk around Ballina Head and down the steps to Lighthouse Beach. At the end of Lighthouse Beach climb up to the North Wall and return to the marine rescue tower.

TERRAIN

Paved path, single track, beach.

CHALLENGES

Sun exposure in summer .

GETTING THERE

Lighthouse Pde is at the southeastern end of East Ballina. Drive to the end of the parade and park.

CAFÉS

Lighthouse Beach Café, The Belle General.

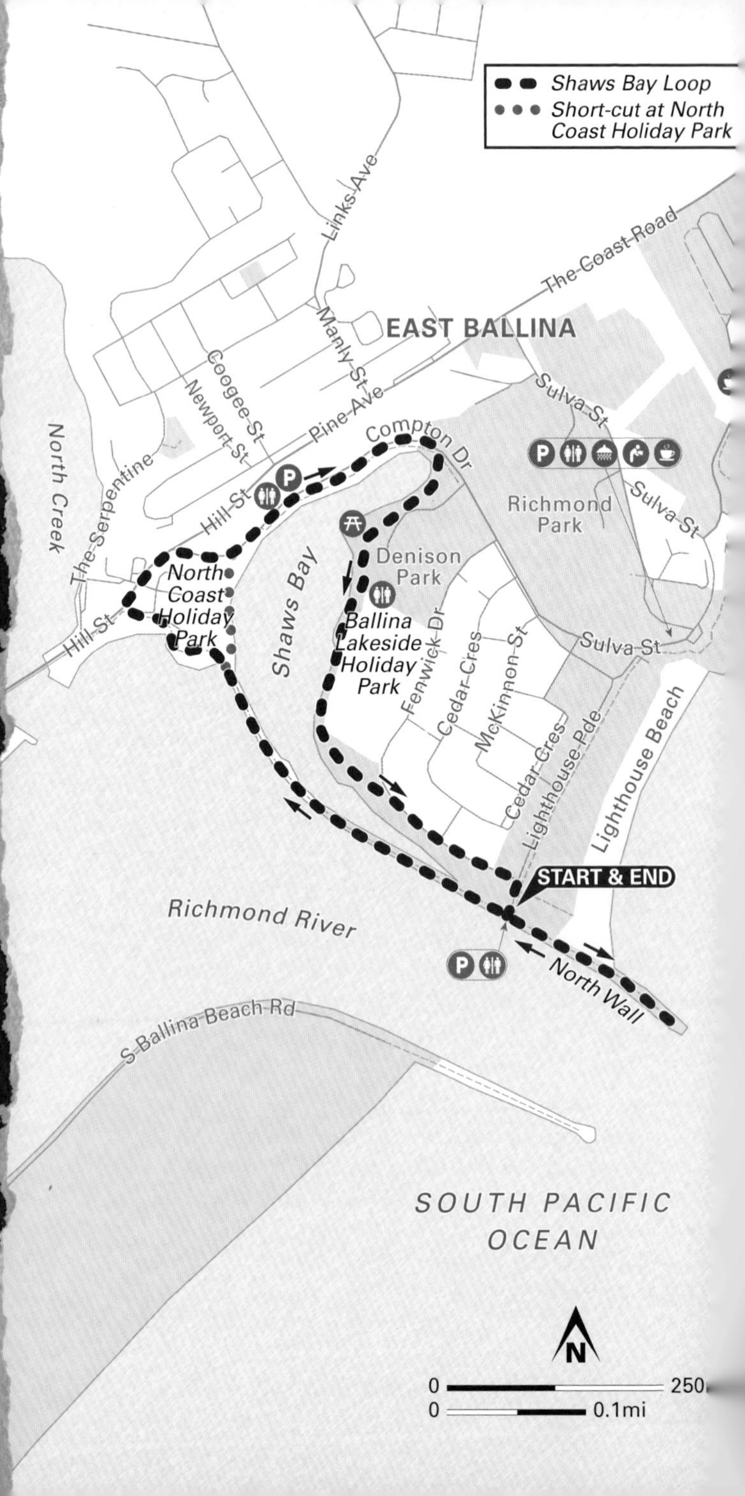

Shaws Bay Loop
Short-cut at North Coast Holiday Park

EAST BALLINA
The Coast Road
Links Ave
Manly St
Coogee St
Newport St
Pine Ave
Compton Dr
Sulva St
Richmond Park
Sulva St
Sulva St
North Creek
The Serpentine
Hill St
Hill St
North Coast Holiday Park
Shaws Bay
Denison Park
Ballina Lakeside Holiday Park
Fenwick Dr
Cedar Cres
McKinnon St
Cedar Cres
Lighthouse Pde
Lighthouse Beach
START & END
Richmond River
North Wall
S Ballina Beach Rd
SOUTH PACIFIC OCEAN

N

0 250
0 0.1mi

Amazing views along the river and the North Wall. Beautiful river beaches. Expansive walk with lots of variety.

TRAILHEAD: Marine rescue tower on Lighthouse Pde

From the marine rescue tower walk left along the North Wall to take in the expansive view of Richmond River meeting the sea. Return to the marine tower and continue along the breakwall to North Coast Holiday Park. Pick up the roadside path on Hill St and follow it onto Compton Dr.

After 2km you reach the edge of Denison Park. Turn right into the park and walk along the grass following the line of trees on the right that skirts Shaws Bay. After the three picnic shelters look for a small track through the bush. Follow the bush track until you come out into a grass clearing, then veer right through more bush towards the water.

Continue along the stretch of park between Shaws Bay and Ballina Lakeside Holiday Park to the wide grassy clearing at the end. Follow the water's edge and the grassy verge between the bay and Fenwick Dr. Fenwick Dr will take you back to Lighthouse Pde and the marine rescue tower.

TERRAIN

Paved path.

CHALLENGES

Sun exposure in summer.

Some roadside walking.

GETTING THERE

Lighthouse Pde is at the southeastern end of East Ballina. Drive to the end of the parade and park.

CAFÉS

Lighthouse Beach Café, The Belle General.

Nightcap National Park & Whian Whian SCA

NATURAL ENVIRONMENT

Nightcap National Park, part of the Gondwana Rainforests of Australia World Heritage Area, is a dramatically beautiful park full of ancient rainforests, magical waterways and spectacular views. The lush rainforest provides a home for the newly discovered nightcap oak as well as a number of threatened animal species, including Albert's lyrebird and Fleay's barred frog, which takes shelter under leaf litter and makes an 'ok-okok-ok-ok' sound after rain. Nightcap National Park sits at the southern rim of the Tweed Volcano caldera and the erosion-resistant rhyolite rock formed the sheer cliffs over which flows Repentance Creek, creating Minyon Falls. Fertile volcanic soil has resulted in some of the best subtropical rainforest you'll ever walk through.

Nightcap National Park was established in 1983 and covers 81 square kilometres. Whian Whian State Conservation Area (SCA) covers 24 square kilometres.

MINYON FALLS, RUMMERY PARK & NIGHTCAP RANGE ROAD AREAS

The walks in these areas of the national park offer the opportunity to experience a range of forests, pristine creeks and a spectacular waterfall along the Nightcap escarpment.

Amid the growth on the upper reaches of the falls you'll find coral fern, sedge, wildflowers, mosses, cedars and mixed gums, and wet sclerophyll forest of tall blackbutt, tallowwood and flooded gum.

Then as you descend into the rainforest you will see large, old, heavily buttressed strangler figs, brush box, coachwood, sassafras and white birch. The valley floor is home to lush bangalow palm forests alongside Repentance Creek. Minyon Falls Flora Reserve contains red cedars, blue figs, bangalow palms and many other old-growth trees. Stream lilies and helmholtzia lilies put out white flowers in summer. Other valley species include rusty rose walnut, blue quandong, broad-leaved palm lily, tree fern, red lilly-pilly, brush box orchid and native wisteria vine.

Some of the wildlife you can expect to encounter are wompoo and wonga pigeons and an assortment of other rainforest pigeons and birds including catbirds, bowerbirds, figbirds, Lewin's honeyeaters, tawny frogmouths, kingfishers and king parrots. Yellow-tailed black cockatoos, wedge-tailed eagles, Pacific bazas and other raptors can be seen at the higher altitudes. Pademelons, koalas and bandicoots can be seen around the picnic areas at dusk or dawn, when you might even spy a sugar, squirrel or yellow-bellied glider. The long-necked turtle and platypus can be found in the creeks along with a variety of frogs.

ROCKY CREEK DAM AREA

The vegetation in the catchment is mainly subtropical rainforest or wet sclerophyll. The subtropical rainforest is generally regarded as one of the biggest remnants of the Big Scrub rainforest that once existed over a large part of the surrounding region.

TERANIA CREEK AREA

The Terania Basin contains the largest and most extensive bangalow palm forest in NSW and is home to such treasures as 1000- to 1200-year-old brush box trees, the vulnerable black-breasted button-quail and the endangered red-legged pademelon. You will often find goannas and kookaburras in the picnic and camping area around meal times and pademelons often appear at sunset.

MT NARDI AREA

Mt Nardi has some of the most beautiful rainforest walks in the Nightcap area. Tall tree ferns, walking stick palms, elkhorns, stags and vines make this a magical walking area, traversing three different forest types. On the southern side of the escarpment the walking track meanders through lush World Heritage–listed tropical rainforest. You will see yellow carabeen and towering brush box as well as a little hollowed-out tree trunk that gathers water and looks like a wishing well. Many different types of unusual fungi and mosses can be found clinging to the stumps of fallen trees. The fungi that have set up in the buttresses of one tree create a larder-shelf effect and it's easy to feel like you're in nature's kitchen! There are lots of ancient-growth trees that have died and given themselves over to the mosses, fungi and other life forms, which have eaten them down to shadows of their former selves.

As you transition over the ridge towards the escarpment edges, the contrast in vegetation is noticeable. Drier vegetation dominates in the rain shadow and gorgeous mature grass trees, giant blackbutt and eucalypts are prolific. Many old-growth trees hang right over the escarpment in various places and make this part of the walk a nature trove.

You might see an Albert's lyrebird in the understorey and they are often heard early in the morning along the track from Newton Dr. Peregrine falcons are sometimes seen surfing the updrafts along this stunning escarpment.

HUONBROOK AREA

The ridges of the Huonbrook area of Nightcap National Park comprise dry sclerophyll blackbutt forest, with ecotonal wet sclerophyll forest dominated by brush box and wet-to-moist sclerophyll forest on the lower slopes. You will find expanding subtropical rainforest in the gullies and sheltered hill slopes. Old-growth eucalypt forest, important habitat for hollow-dependent threatened fauna species such as the sooty owl, can be found in several places throughout the area.

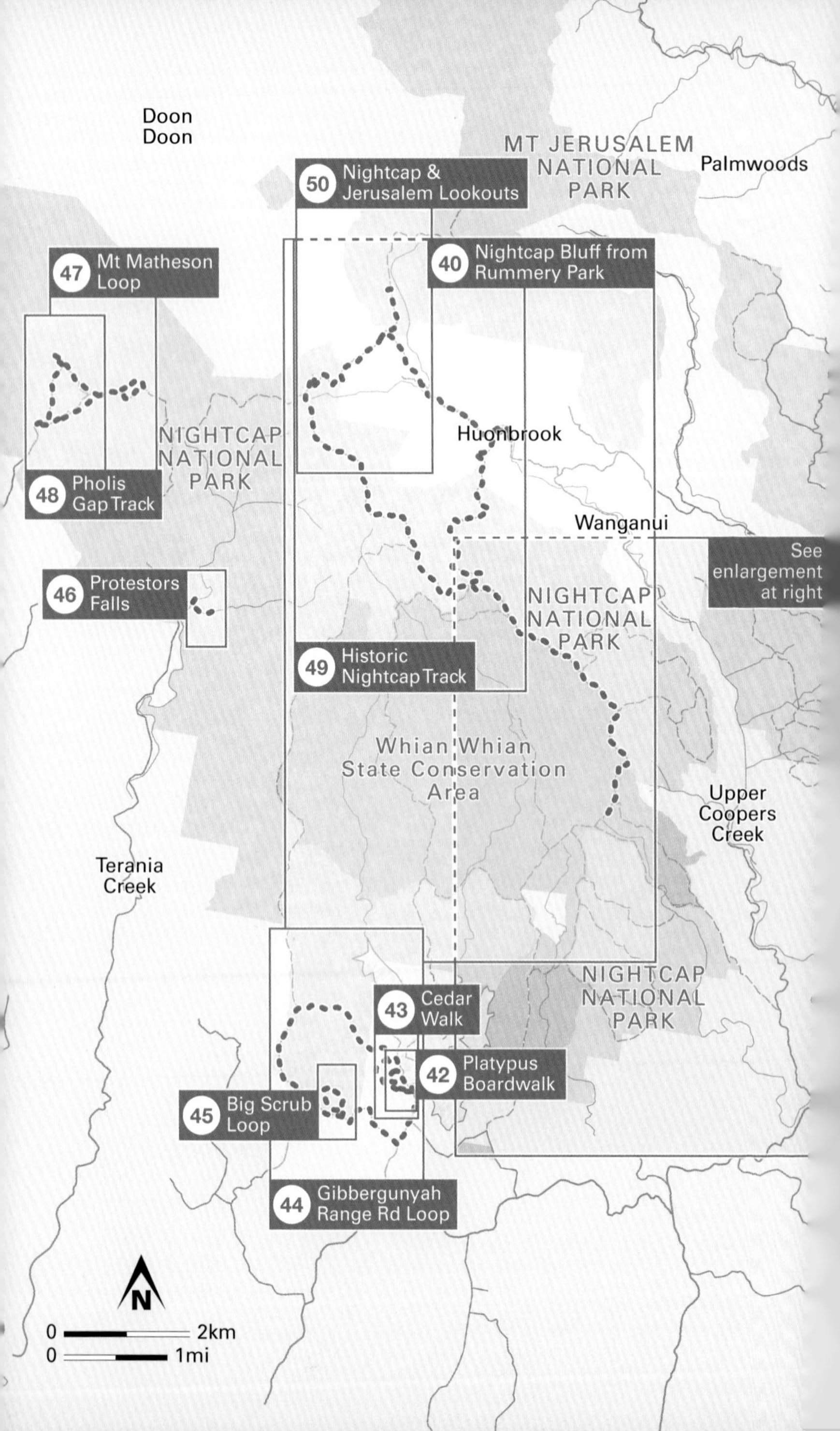

Doon Doon
MT JERUSALEM NATIONAL PARK
Palmwoods
50 Nightcap & Jerusalem Lookouts
47 Mt Matheson Loop
40 Nightcap Bluff from Rummery Park
Huonbrook
NIGHTCAP NATIONAL PARK
48 Pholis Gap Track
Wanganui
See enlargement at right
46 Protestors Falls
NIGHTCAP NATIONAL PARK
49 Historic Nightcap Track
Whian Whian State Conservation Area
Upper Coopers Creek
Terania Creek
NIGHTCAP NATIONAL PARK
43 Cedar Walk
42 Platypus Boardwalk
45 Big Scrub Loop
44 Gibbergunyah Range Rd Loop
N
0 2km
0 1mi

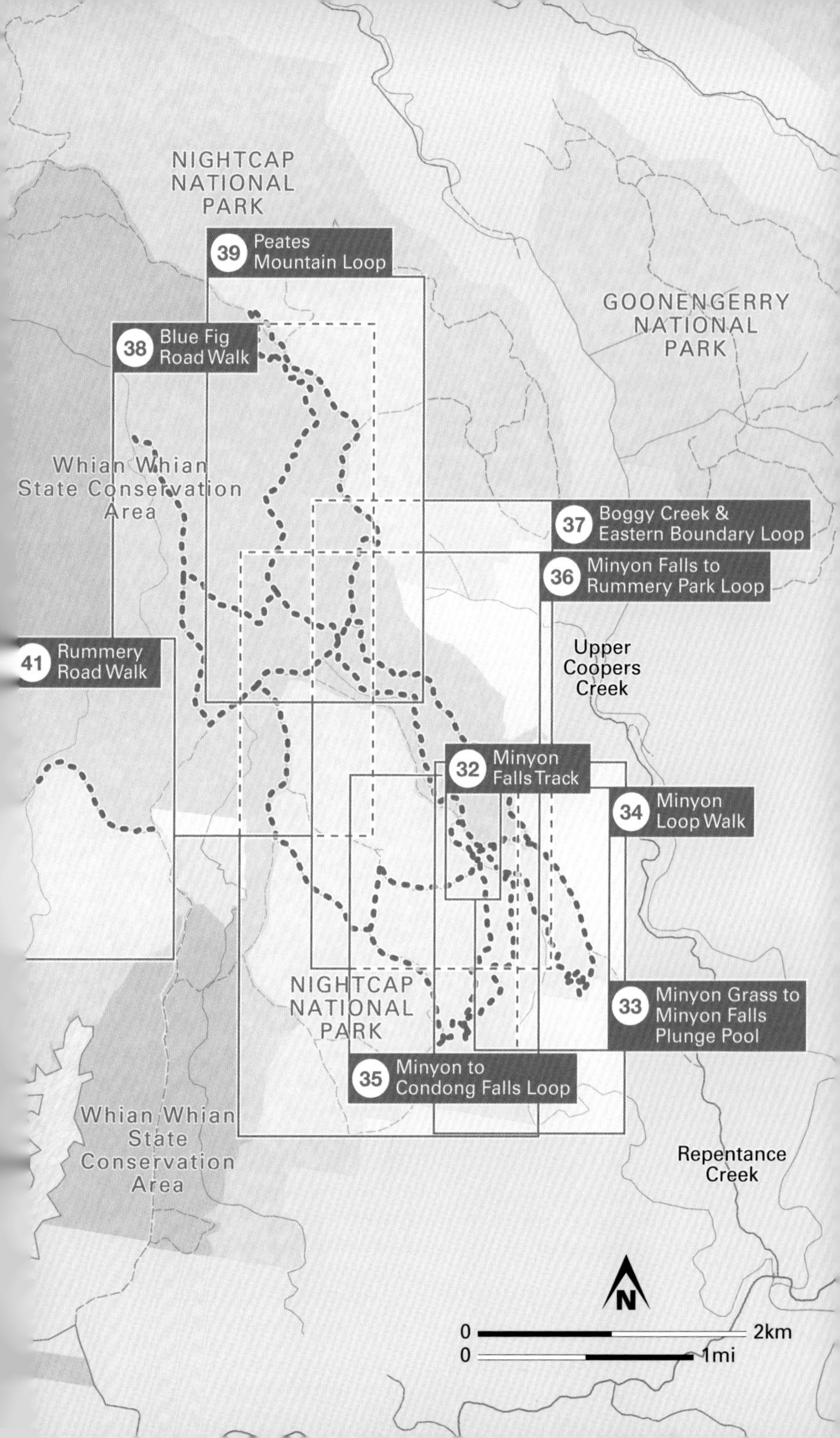

NIGHTCAP NATIONAL PARK
39 Peates Mountain Loop
38 Blue Fig Road Walk
GOONENGERRY NATIONAL PARK
Whian Whian State Conservation Area
37 Boggy Creek & Eastern Boundary Loop
36 Minyon Falls to Rummery Park Loop
41 Rummery Road Walk
Upper Coopers Creek
32 Minyon Falls Track
34 Minyon Loop Walk
NIGHTCAP NATIONAL PARK
33 Minyon Grass to Minyon Falls Plunge Pool
35 Minyon to Condong Falls Loop
Whian Whian State Conservation Area
Repentance Creek
N
0
2km
0
1mi

Getting to Nightcap National Park and Whian Whian SCA

There are five public-access roads into Nightcap National Park and Whian Whian State Conservation Area from the south:

- Minyon Falls Rd (To Minyon Falls and Rummery Park)
- Nightcap Range Rd (To Rummery Rd)
- Rocky Creek Dam Rd (To Rocky Creek Dam)
- Terania Creek Rd (To Protestors Falls)
- Tuntable Creek Rd (To Mt Nardi)

Minyon Falls Rd, Nightcap Range Rd and Terania Creek Rd are 2WD unsealed dirt roads and be rough at times. The roads around this part of the area can be confusing so use GPS if you have it. There is one private-access road into the park from the northeastern side, which is used for the Historic Nightcap Track.

If there has been heavy rain or recent storms check for road or trail closures before you head out there. Nightcap area has the highest annual rainfall in NSW, so you may get caught in the rain. Be prepared.

GETTING TO MINYON FALLS AREA

From Goonengerry (to the north), head south on Federal Rd. After 1.5km turn right onto Repentance Creek Rd. After 4.6km turn right onto Upper Coopers Creek Rd.

From Rosebank (to the south), head north on Rosebank Rd. After 1.9km continue onto Repentance Creek Rd. 4.8km along Repentance Creek Rd turn left onto Upper Coopers Creek Rd.

Upper Coopers Creek Rd turns left and becomes Minyon Falls Rd. The Minyon Falls picnic area and car park are 2.2km along this road. The road is unsealed.

GETTING TO RUMMERY PARK CAMPING AREA

From Goonengerry (to the north), head south on Federal Rd. After 1.5km turn right onto Repentance Creek Rd. After 4.6km turn right onto Upper Coopers Creek Rd.

From Rosebank (to the south), head north on Rosebank Rd. After 1.9km continue onto Repentance Creek Rd. 4.8km along Repentance Creek Rd turn left onto Upper Coopers Creek Rd.

Upper Coopers Creek Rd turns left and becomes Minyon Falls Rd. The road is unsealed. At the end of Minyon Falls Rd turn right onto Peates Mountain Rd and park at the camping ground.

GETTING TO NIGHTCAP RANGE ROAD & RUMMERY ROAD

From Goonengerry (to the north), head south on Federal Rd. After 1.5km turn right onto Repentance Creek Rd. After 8.5km turn sharp right onto Dunoon Rd. 3.4km along this road is the right turn for Nightcap Range Rd.

From Rosebank (to the south), head north on Rosebank Rd. After 1.9km continue onto Repentance Creek Rd. 1km along Repentance Creek Rd turn slight left onto Dunoon Rd. After 3.4km turn right onto Nightcap Range Rd.

Once on Nightcap Range Rd you enter Whian Whian SCA after 2.2km. Drive or walk 3.2km to reach Rummery Rd.

GETTING TO ROCKY CREEK DAM

From Goonengerry (to the north), head south on Federal Rd. After 1.5km turn right onto Repentance Creek Rd. After 8.5km turn sharp right onto Dunoon Rd. 6.6km along this road is the right turn for Rocky Creek Dam Rd.

From Rosebank (to the south), head north on Rosebank Rd. After 1.9km continue onto Repentance Creek Rd. 1km along Repentance Creek Rd turn slight left onto Dunoon Rd. At 6.6km along this road is the left turn for Rocky Creek Dam Rd.

About 1.5km along this road is a left turn for Gibbergunyah Range Rd. Rocky Creek Dam is 900m further along Rocky Creek Dam Rd.

GETTING TO TERANIA CREEK

From The Channon take Mill St out of town. Mill St becomes Terania Creek Rd. Drive for 14.5km along Terania Creek Rd to reach Terania Creek picnic area. This is a slow-going, mostly unsealed road.

GETTING TO MT NARDI

From The Channon drive north out of town on Tuntable Creek Rd. After 12.5km take the right turn for Newton Dr. Drive for 6.7km to the end of Newton Dr and park on the road to the right close to the information shelter.

GETTING TO HUONBROOK

5km northwest of Wilson's Creek on Wilson's Creek Rd is a fork in the road. Turn left for Huonbrook. After 1.7km keep left to stay on Huonbrook Rd. After 1.2km turn right to stay on Huonbrook Rd: 2.9km along this road is a gate to your right with a sign saying 'No vehicles, walkers only'. Park here. Beware of the deep ditch close to the road and do not obstruct access to the gate.

This gate marks the start of Red Rd, which is a private road, however the owners graciously allow access. Please respect their property.

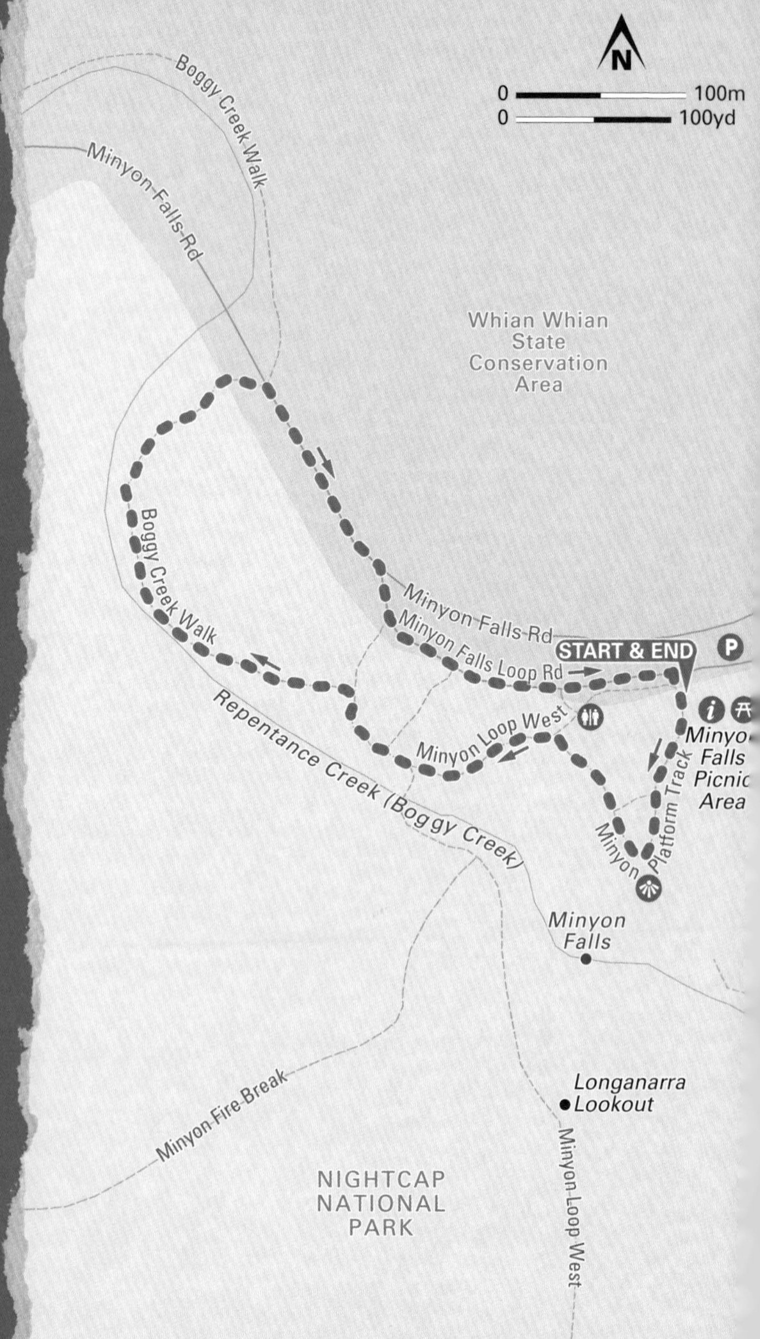
N
0 100m
0 100yd
Boggy Creek Walk
Minyon Falls Rd
Whian Whian State Conservation Area
Boggy Creek Walk
Minyon Falls Rd
Minyon Falls Loop Rd
START & END
P
Minyon Loop West
Repentance Creek (Boggy Creek)
Minyon Falls Picnic Area
Minyon Platform Track
Minyon
Minyon Falls
Longanarra Lookout
Minyon Fire Break
NIGHTCAP NATIONAL PARK
Minyon Loop West

This easy walk takes you the top of Minyon Falls. It is especially good after lots of rain.

TRAILHEAD: Minyon Falls picnic area

From the Minyon Falls parking and picnic area walk along the paved path to the viewing platform that overlooks Minyon Falls. The falls are 100m high and have formed from the waters of Repentance Creek flowing over erosion-resistant rhyolite rock cliffs that were once part of the Tweed Volcano.

From there walk upstream along the boardwalk, i.e. take the path to the left coming from the platform. Continue upstream along the walking track as it skirts Repentance Creek. Keep left ignoring the forks that lead right to the road. Eventually you will emerge onto Minyon Falls Rd and the junction with Boggy Creek Walk. Turn right and walk along Minyon Falls Rd which returns to Minyon Falls car park and picnic area.

TERRAIN

Boardwalk, unsealed road.

CHALLENGES

Possibility of puddles and leeches after heavy rainfall.

GETTING THERE

See pg 120.

CAFÉS

Doma Café Federal, The Rosebank Store, Crystal Castle.

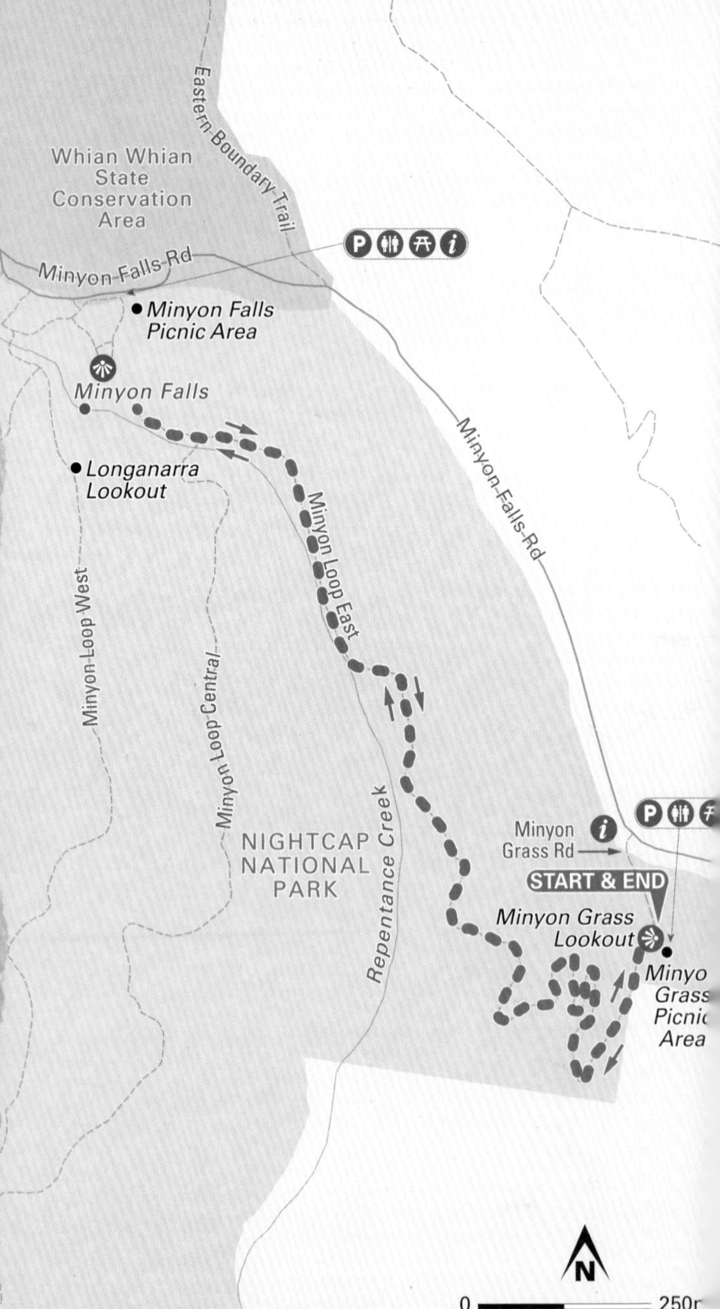

Whian Whian State Conservation Area
Eastern Boundary Trail
Minyon Falls Rd
Minyon Falls Picnic Area
Minyon Falls
Longanarra Lookout
Minyon Loop East
Minyon Loop West
Minyon Loop Central
Minyon Falls Rd
NIGHTCAP NATIONAL PARK
Repentance Creek
Minyon Grass Rd
START & END
Minyon Grass Lookout
Minyo Grass Picnic Area
N
0
250m
0
0.1mi

Minyon Grass offers the best views of Minyon Falls. It's nice to swim in the plunge pool in summer, but don't wear sunscreen or repellent if you intend to. Sturdy walking shoes needed. Walking stick helpful.

TRAILHEAD: Minyon Grass Viewing Platform

From the picnic area head downhill along the walking track which switches back on itself as it descends into the valley. After about 1km of steep downhill grade the path levels out somewhat and continues for another 1km until it reaches Repentance Creek. Just before the creek is a path to the right leading upstream to the plunge pool and the base of Minyon Falls. The path eventually peters out and the last section becomes a rock scramble to reach the pool. It is not marked and easy to miss so ask other walkers for directions if you're uncertain.

To return to Minyon Grass picnic area retrace your steps over the rocks and back onto the walking track. Turn left at the creek and follow the track uphill for the 2km climb.

TERRAIN

Single track, some steep sections.

CHALLENGES

Steep descent.

Consider not using repellent or sunscreen if you plan to swim.

Muddy track and leeches after rain.

The rainforest gets dark quickly – leave enough daylight to complete.

GETTING THERE

See pg 120.

CAFÉS

Doma Café Federal, The Rosebank Store, Crystal Castle.

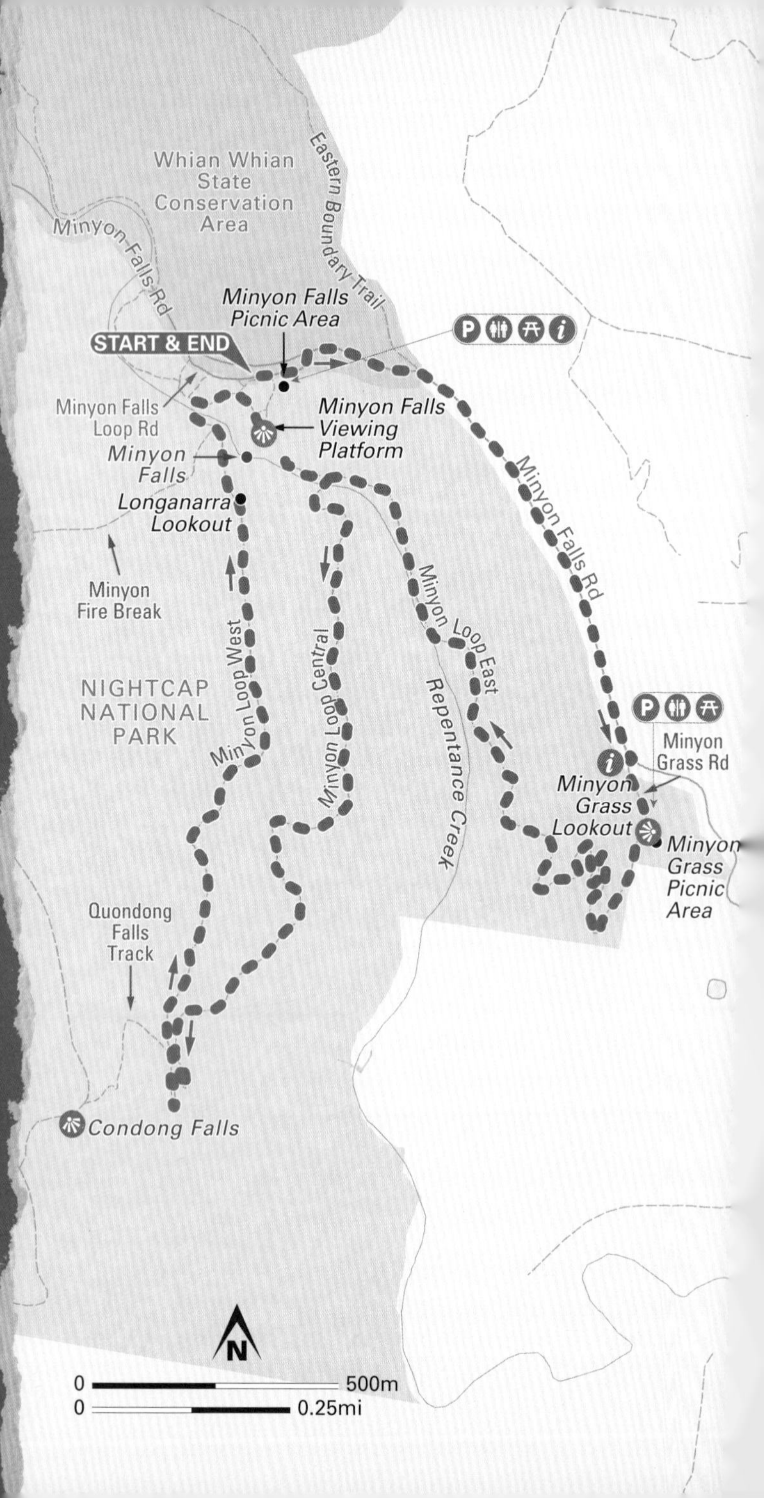

Whian Whian State Conservation Area

Eastern Boundary Trail

Minyon Falls Rd

Minyon Falls Picnic Area

START & END

Minyon Falls Loop Rd

Minyon Falls Viewing Platform

Minyon Falls

Longanarra Lookout

Minyon Fire Break

Minyon Falls Rd

Minyon Loop East

Repentance Creek

Minyon Loop Central

Minyon Loop West

NIGHTCAP NATIONAL PARK

Minyon Grass Rd

Minyon Grass Lookout

Minyon Grass Picnic Area

Quondong Falls Track

Condong Falls

N

0 500m

0 0.25mi

P

Takes in Minyon Grass and Minyon Falls from above and below. Great day hike. Sturdy walking shoes needed. Walking stick helpful.

TRAILHEAD: Minyon Falls picnic area car park

Walk downhill along the road you drove in by. At the information shelter take Minyon Grass Rd to the right.

Take the signposted walking track from Minyon Grass picnic area. The track switches back on itself as it descends into the valley. After 1km of steep descent the track levels out and continues for another 1km to Repentance Creek. Just before the creek take the unmarked path to the right leading upstream to the plunge pool and the base of Minyon Falls. The last section is a rock scramble to reach the pool.

Retrace your steps to Minyon Loop track. Turn right and cross the creek. The track climbs steadily and then steeply through large old-growth trees. Again it switches back on itself and at one point offers views of Condong Falls to the west.

At the fork and turn-off for Quandong Falls Track, keep right to stay on Minyon Loop track. The track travels along the top of the escarpment climbing gradually through large old escarpment trees and offers some views of Minyon Falls. At the junction with Minyon Fire Break continue straight and cross Repentance Creek. Keep right at the next two forks and follow the path to the Minyon Falls viewing platform.

TERRAIN

Single track, some steep sections.

CHALLENGES

Steep descent.

Muddy track and leeches after rain.

The rainforest gets dark quickly – leave enough daylight to complete.

GETTING THERE

See pg 120.

CAFÉS

Doma Café Federal, The Rosebank Store, Crystal Castle.

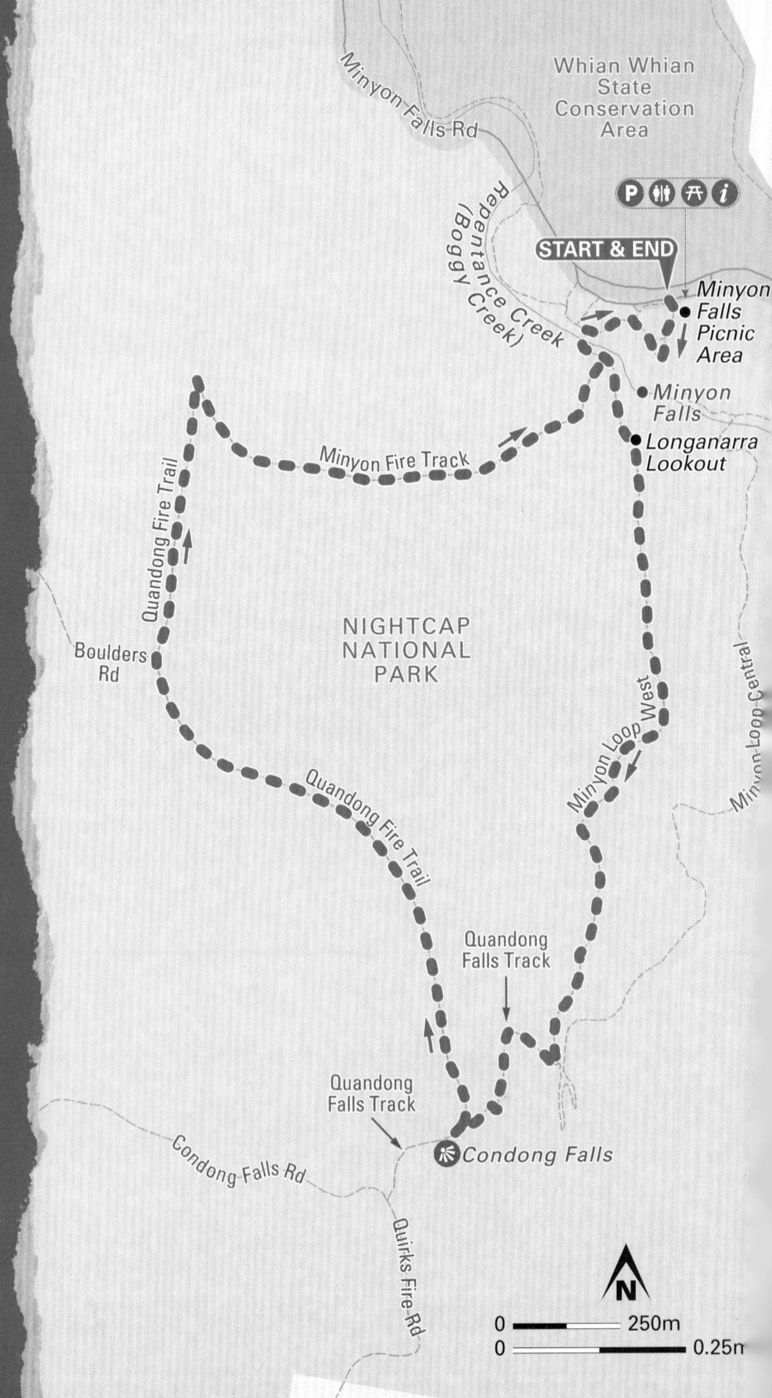
Minyon Falls Rd
Whian Whian State Conservation Area
START & END
Repentance Creek (Boggy Creek)
Minyon Falls Picnic Area
Minyon Falls
Longanarra Lookout
Minyon Fire Track
Quandong Fire Trail
Boulders Rd
NIGHTCAP NATIONAL PARK
Minyon Loop West
Minyon Loop Central
Quandong Fire Trail
Quandong Falls Track
Quandong Falls Track
Condong Falls
Condong Falls Rd
Quirks Fire Rd
N
0 250m
0 0.25m

Waterfall and ridge-top views. Pools at the top of Condong Falls. Sturdy walking shoes needed.

TRAILHEAD: Minyon Falls picnic area car park

Walk to the viewing platform overlooking Minyon Falls. After soaking up the view, take the boardwalk to the left and continue veering left until you reach the permanent stepping stones that cross the creek. The path climbs and reaches a fork. Keep left along Minyon Loop track. The track travels along the top of the escarpment descending gradually through large old escarpment trees and offers some views of Minyon Falls. It then forks at the turn-off for Quandong Falls Track. Keep right. After 300m you reach Quandong Fire Trail. Turn left. Condong Creek is immediately in front of you with Condong Falls to the left.

There are some views of the valley below from the top of the falls. This is a nice place to sit and watch for soaring eagles or rainforest birds, or to take a dip in the pools.

To return, retrace your steps from the creek. Ignore the right turn for Quandong Falls Track and continue along Quandong Fire Trail. After 1.2km the road forks (for Boulders Rd). Keep right to stay on Quandong Fire Trail. After 500m the road forks again. Turn right for the Minyon Fire Break trail. After 900m you return to Minyon Loop trail. Turn left, cross the Repentance Creek stepping stones and turn right for Minyon Falls picnic area.

TERRAIN

Single track, fire trail.

CHALLENGES

Sheer cliff edge at waterfall.

Consider not using repellent or sunscreen if you plan to swim.

Muddy track and leeches after rain.

The rainforest gets dark quickly – leave enough daylight to complete.

GETTING THERE

See pg 120.

CAFÉS

Doma Café Federal, The Rosebank Store, Crystal Castle.

Minyon Falls to Rummery Park Loop

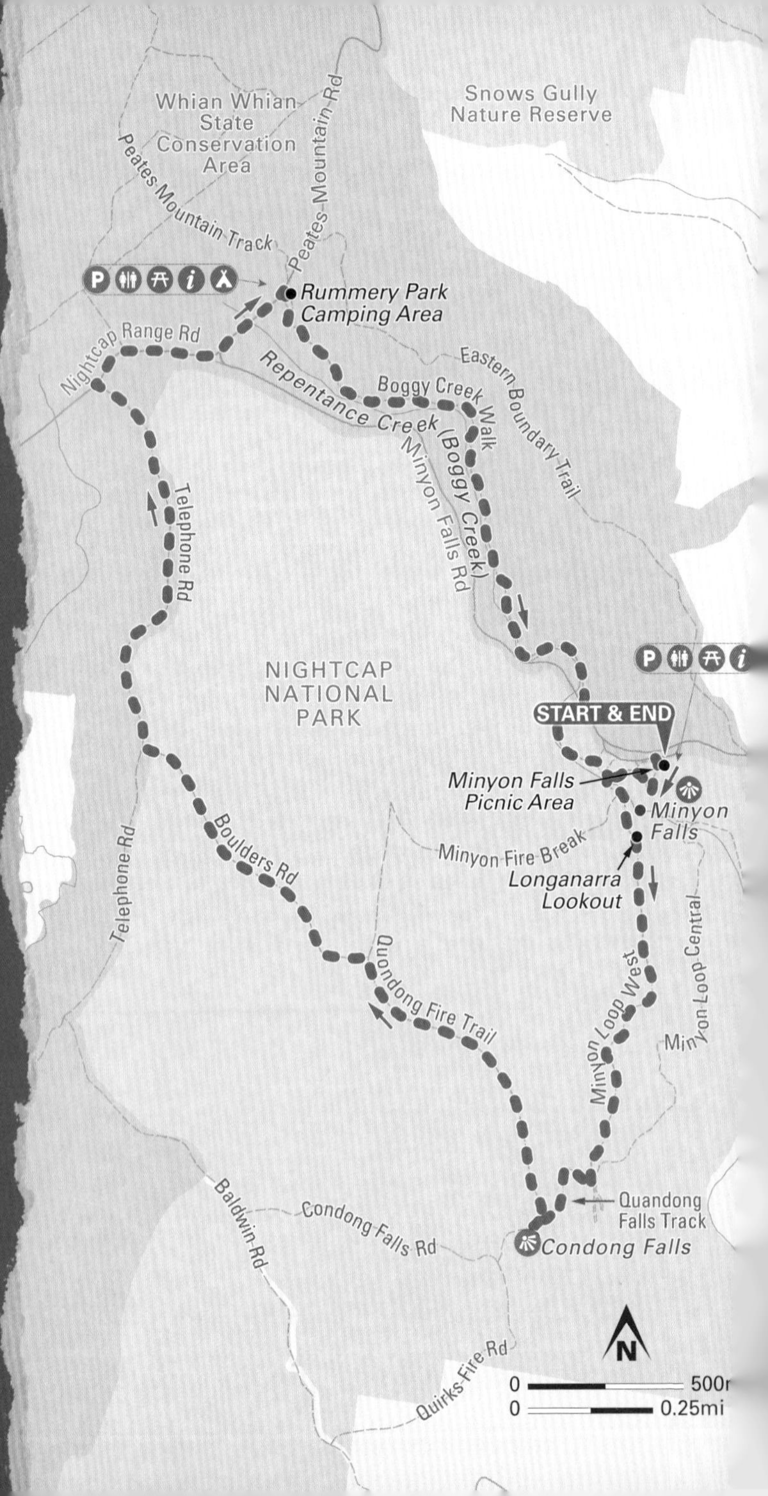

P
i

Whian Whian State Conservation Area
Snows Gully Nature Reserve
Peates Mountain Rd
Peates Mountain Track
Rummery Park Camping Area
Nightcap Range Rd
Repentance Creek
Boggy Creek Walk
Eastern Boundary Trail
Minyon Falls Rd
(Boggy Creek)
Telephone Rd
NIGHTCAP NATIONAL PARK
START & END
Minyon Falls Picnic Area
Minyon Falls
Minyon Fire Break
Longanarra Lookout
Boulders Rd
Quondong Fire Trail
Minyon Loop West
Minyon Loop Central
Quandong Falls Track
Condong Falls
Condong Falls Rd
Baldwin Rd
Quirks Fire Rd
N
0 500m
0 0.25mi

Waterfall views. Pools along Boggy Creek. Sturdy walking shoes needed.

TRAILHEAD: Minyon Falls picnic area

Walk to the viewing platform overlooking Minyon Falls. After soaking up the view, take the boardwalk to the left and continue veering left until you reach the permanent stepping stones that cross the creek. The path climbs and reaches a fork. Keep left along Minyon Loop track. The track travels along the top of the escarpment descending gradually through large old escarpment trees and offers some views of Minyon Falls. The track forks at the turn-off for Quandong Falls Track. Take this right turn. After 300m you reach Quandong Fire Trail. Turn left. Condong Creek is immediately in front of you with Condong Falls to the left.

To return, retrace your steps from the creek. Ignore the right turn for Quandong Falls Track and continue along Quandong Fire Trail. After 1.2km the road forks. Turn left for Boulders Rd. Turn right at the next fork with Telephone Rd. After 1.3km turn right onto Nightcap Range Rd. Keep left at the three-way junction onto Peates Mountain Rd and Rummery Park Camping Area.

Turn right and walk to the end of the camping oval to pick up Boggy Creek Trail, an easy meandering track along Repentance Creek (known as Boggy Creek along this section). Small side tracks lead down to creek pools. The trail crosses over Minyon Falls Rd and continues along the creek to the picnic area.

TERRAIN

Single track, fire trail.

CHALLENGES

Sheer cliff edge at waterfall.

Consider not using repellent or sunscreen if you plan to swim.

Muddy track and leeches after rain.

The rainforest gets dark quickly – leave enough daylight to complete.

GETTING THERE

See pg 120.

CAFÉS

Doma Café Federal, The Rosebank Store, Crystal Castle.

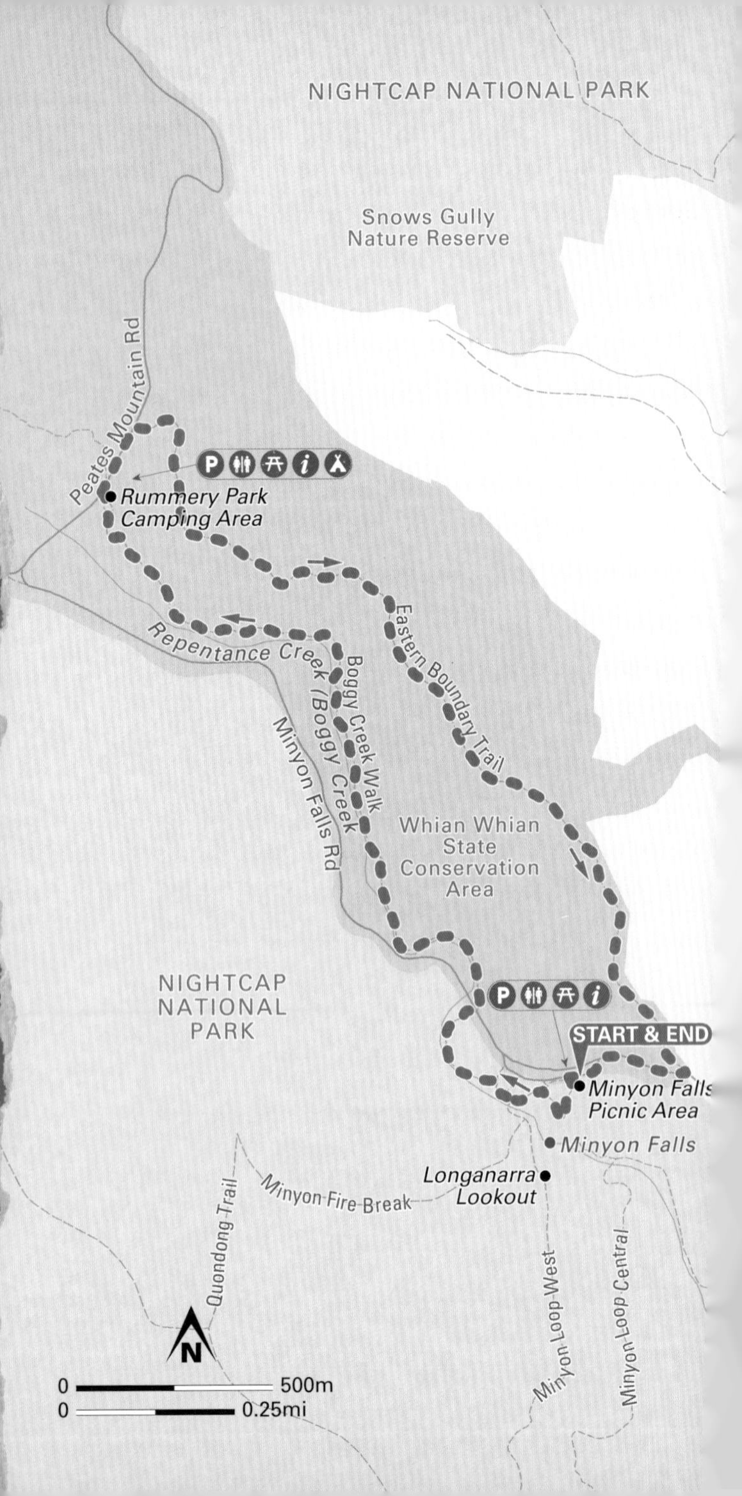

NIGHTCAP NATIONAL PARK
Snows Gully
Nature Reserve
Peates Mountain Rd
Rummery Park
Camping Area
Eastern Boundary Trail
Repentance Creek
Boggy Creek Walk
(Boggy Creek
Minyon Falls Rd
Whian Whian
State
Conservation
Area
NIGHTCAP
NATIONAL
PARK
START & END
Minyon Falls
Picnic Area
Minyon Falls
Longanarra
Lookout
Minyon Fire Break
Quondong Trail
Minyon Loop West
Minyon Loop Central
N
0 500m
0 0.25mi
P

Waterfall view, creekscapes, ridge views. Walking shoes needed.

TRAILHEAD: Minyon Falls picnic area car park

From the viewing platform take the boardwalk to the left. Continue along the path keeping the creek to your left. The trail eventually crosses Minyon Falls Rd and continues to skirt the creek on the far side of the road. This section of Repentence Creek is known as Boggy Creek. There are some small side tracks to the left leading down to rocky creek slabs and creek pools, which offer a good opportunity for a cooling swim. After 2.5km the trail takes you into Rummery Park Camping Area. This is a good spot for a break.

Walk north from the campground and through the gate on Peates Mountain Rd. After 200m take the Eastern Boundary Trail to the right. This trail offers an interesting contrast to the creekside trail. It climbs 60m and then descends 60m before levelling out for a stretch. About 650m from the end of the trail you reach the top of a ridge which offers views of Coopers Creek Valley in the foreground and Byron Bay on the coast. From the ridge the track descends steeply. At the end of the Eastern Boundary Trail you emerge onto Minyon Falls Rd. Take a right and walk the 350m back to Minyon Falls picnic area.

TERRAIN

Single track, fire trail.

CHALLENGES

Muddy track and leeches after rain.

Consider not using repellent or sunscreen if you plan to swim.

GETTING THERE

See pg 120.

CAFÉS

Doma Café Federal, The Rosebank Store, Crystal Castle.

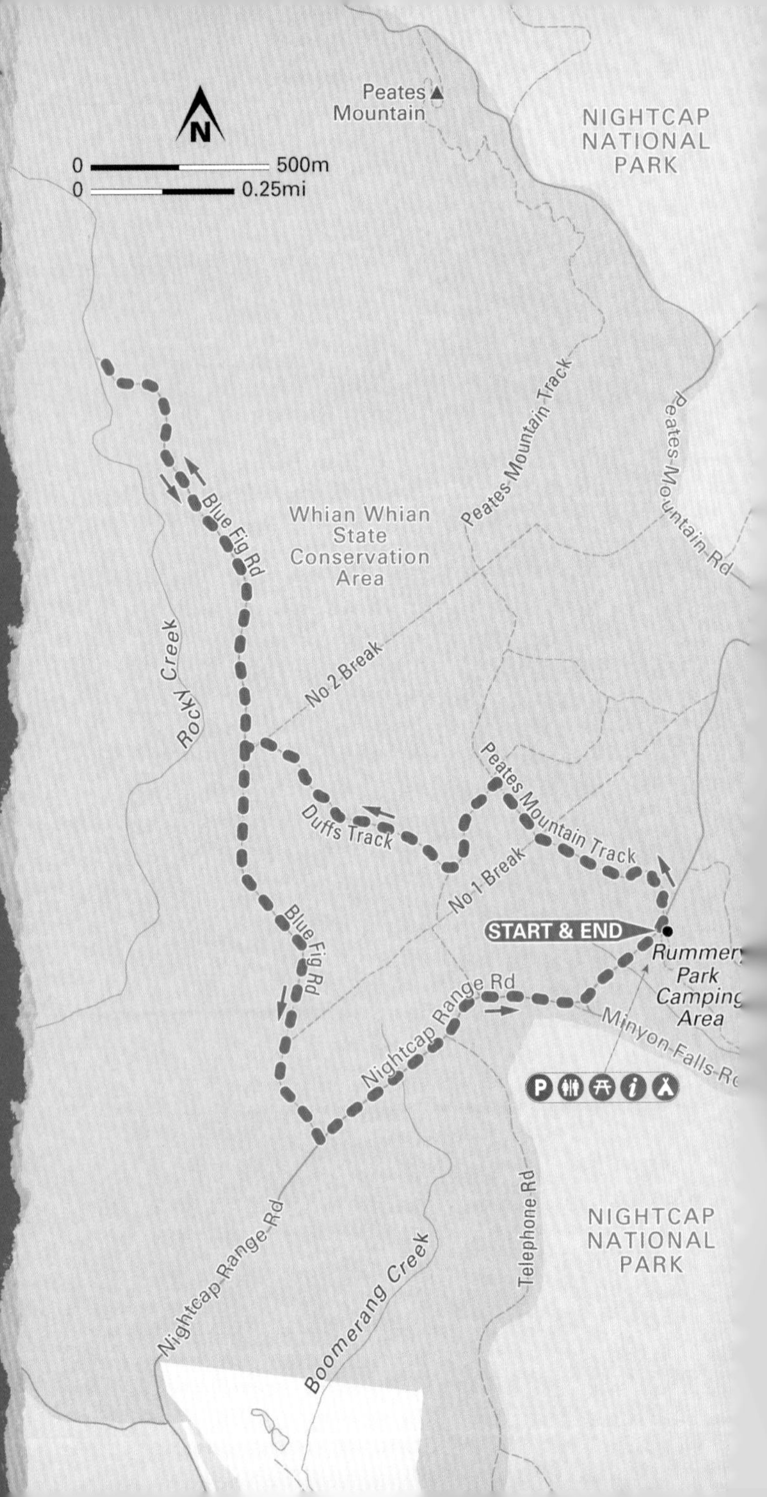

Peates Mountain

NIGHTCAP NATIONAL PARK

0 500m

0 0.25mi

Whian Whian State Conservation Area

Peates Mountain Track

Peates-Mountain-Rd

Blue Fig Rd

Rocky Creek

No 2 Break

Duffs Track

Peates Mountain Track

No 1 Break

START & END

Rummery Park Camping Area

Blue Fig Rd

Nightcap Range Rd

Minyon-Falls-Rd

Nightcap-Range-Rd

Boomerang Creek

Telephone Rd

NIGHTCAP NATIONAL PARK

Beautiful creekscape and rocky cascade where the track reaches Rocky Creek. Further downstream is the Rocky Creek crossing on Rummery Rd. Walking shoes needed.

TRAILHEAD: Rummery Park Camping Area

Walk north from the campground towards the gate on Peates Mountain Rd where you will see a track to the left with a sign for Peates Mountain Track. Take this track. After 25 mins (1.7km) you reach a four-way junction with a trail marker on the left. Turn left here. This track wanders through some open canopy forest and eventually emerges onto Blue Fig Rd. Turn right, go through the gate and walk 20 mins (1.4km) to where the road crosses Rocky Creek. This is a lovely spot to sit, take a rest and take in the creekscape and surroundings.

To return, retrace your steps down Blue Fig Rd. After the gate continue straight along Blue Fig Rd. Once you reach the T-junction with Nightcap Range Rd turn left. At the next major junction turn left again and and follow Peates Mountain Rd back to Rummery Park Camping Area.

TERRAIN

Single track, fire trail.

CHALLENGES

Muddy track and leeches after rain.

GETTING THERE

See pg 120.

CAFÉS

Doma Café Federal, The Rosebank Store, Crystal Castle.

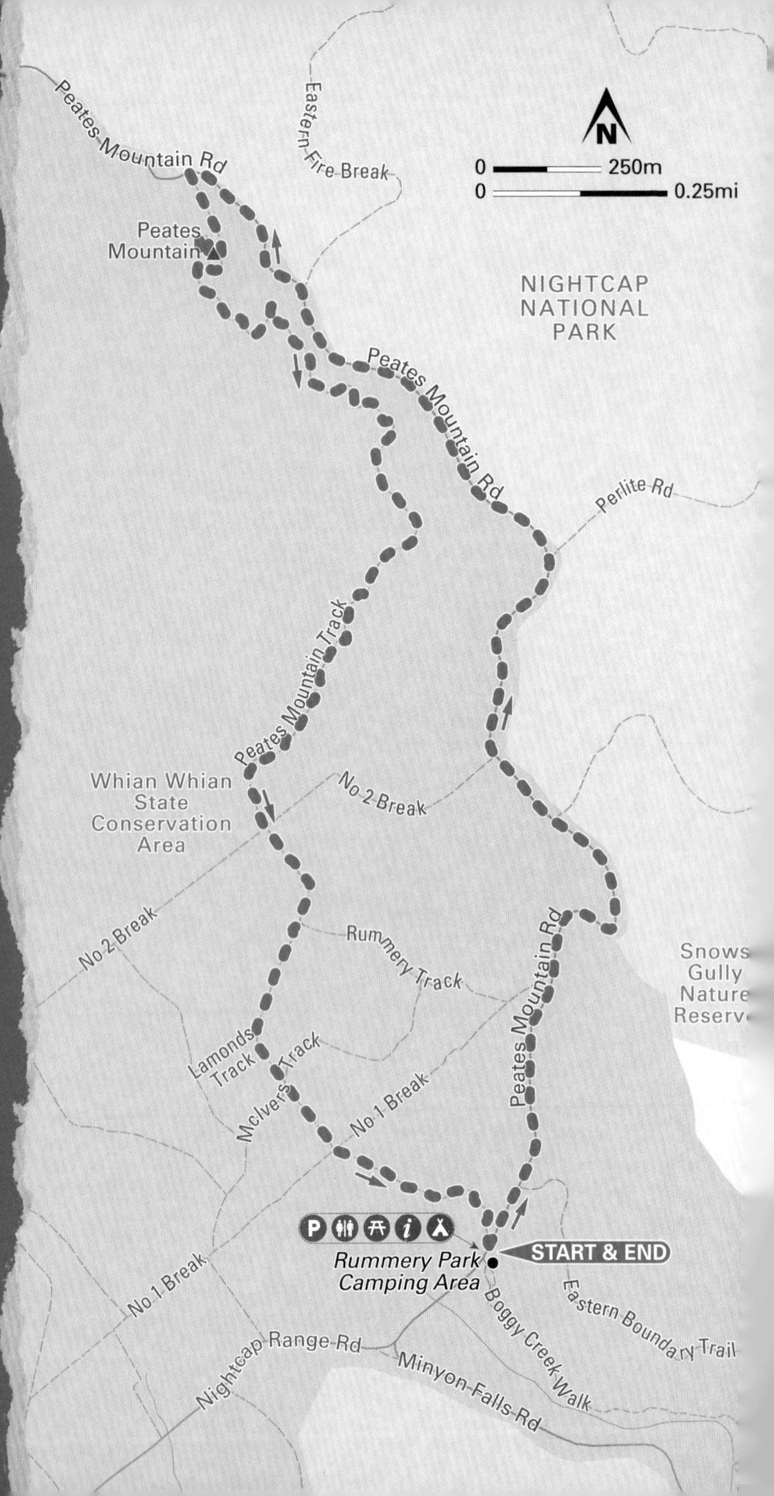

39

Peates Mountain Loop

P

Peates Mountain Rd
Eastern Fire Break
0 250m
0 0.25mi
Peates Mountain
NIGHTCAP NATIONAL PARK
Peates Mountain Rd
Perlite Rd
Peates Mountain Track
Whian Whian State Conservation Area
No 2 Break
No 2 Break
Rummery Track
Peates Mountain Rd
Snows Gully Nature Reserve
Lamonds Track
McIvers Track
No 1 Break
START & END
Rummery Park Camping Area
No 1 Break
Boggy Creek Walk
Eastern Boundary Trail
Nightcap Range Rd
Minyon Falls Rd

Spring and summer see wildflowers such as the nightcap daisy and the white Christmas orchid which flowers in February. Sturdy walking shoes needed.

TRAILHEAD: Rummery Park Camping Area

Walk north from the campground through the gate on Peates Mountain Rd. The fire trail is easy to follow and gradually climbs for over 3km. 400m after Eastern Fire Break trail to your right, a track diverges sharply to your left off Peates Mountain Rd. This track takes you to the top of Peates Mountain (604m).

The top of Peates Mountain was considered a lookout point many years ago, offering views of the surrounding valleys and countryside to the south, east and north. However with increasing forest regrowth these views are becoming limited. You will find a placard close to the top that gives information on the mountain and a plaque denoting the four directions.

The track descends steeply downhill for 400m through blackbutt forest before descending more gradually into rainforest. It crosses several fire trails, No.2 Break, Rummery Track, Lamonds Track, McIvers Track and No.1 Break, and traverses areas of previous heavy logging as well as richer areas of bangalow palm. Once you cross the steel bridge over Boggy Creek, Rummery Park Camping Area is not far.

TERRAIN

Fire trail, single track, some steep sections.

CHALLENGES

Muddy track and leeches after rain.

The rainforest gets dark quickly – leave enough daylight to complete.

GETTING THERE

See pg 120.

CAFÉS

Doma Café Federal, The Rosebank Store, Crystal Castle.

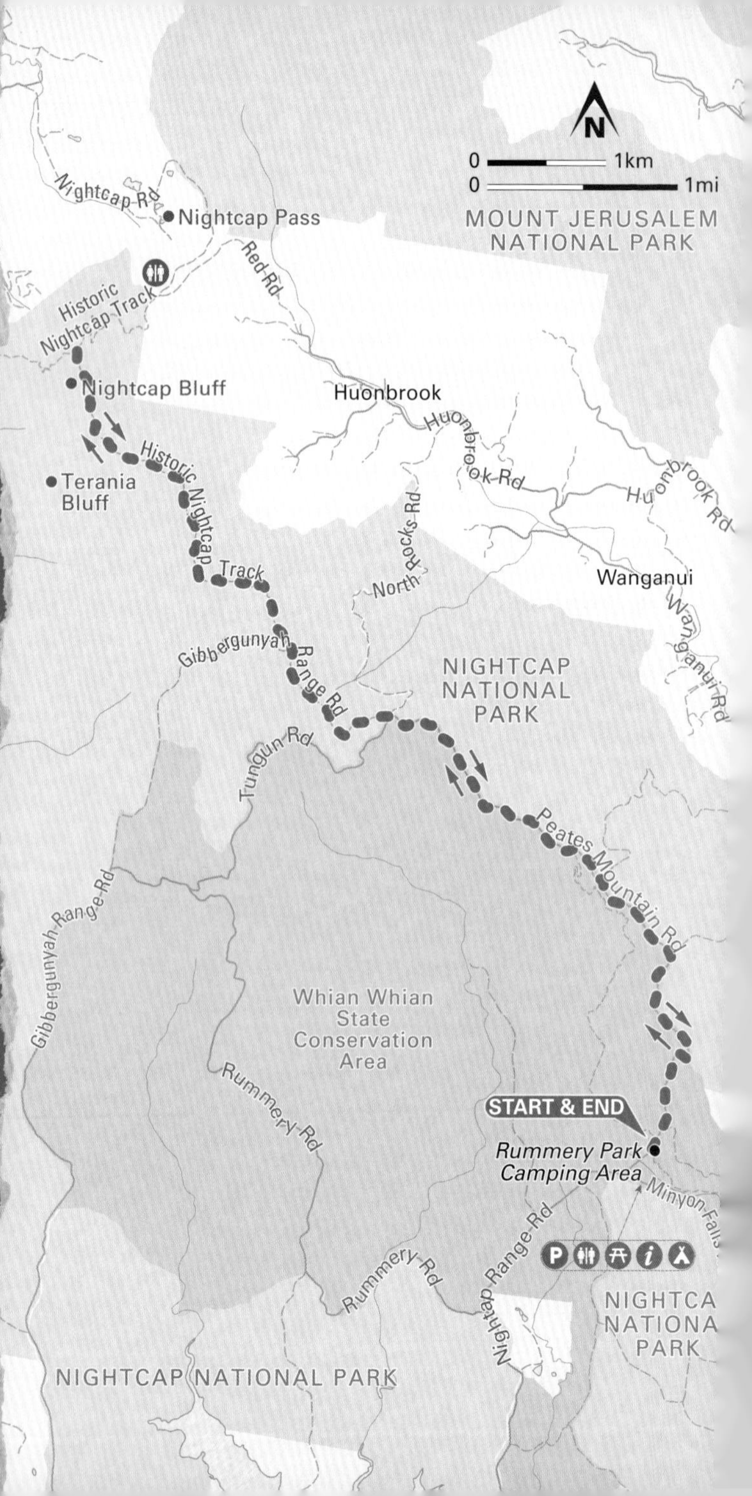

Nightcap Rd
Nightcap Pass
Red Rd
Historic Nightcap Track
Nightcap Bluff
Terania Bluff
Historic Nightcap Track
Huonbrook
Huonbrook Rd
Huonbrook Rd
North Rocks Rd
Wanganui
Wanganui Rd
MOUNT JERUSALEM NATIONAL PARK
0 1km
0 1mi
Gibbergunyah Range Rd
Tungun Rd
NIGHTCAP NATIONAL PARK
Peates Mountain Rd
Gibbergunyah Range Rd
Whian Whian State Conservation Area
Rummery Rd
START & END
Rummery Park Camping Area
Minyon Falls
Nightcap Range Rd
Rummery Rd
NIGHTCAP NATIONAL PARK
NIGHTCAP NATIONAL PARK

Along the Historic Nightcap Track. Views from Nightcap Bluff. Sturdy walking shoes needed Walking stick recommended.

TRAILHEAD: Rummery Park Camping Area

Walk north from the campground through the gate on Peates Mountain Rd. The fire trail is easy to follow and gradually climbs for over 5.5km where it reaches a four-way junction (Peates Mountain Rd, Tungun Rd, Gibbergunyah Range Rd and North Rocks Rd). Walk through the gate onto Gibbergunyah Range Rd. After 45 mins (1.4km) turn right at the signpost for the Historic Nightcap Track on your right. The track climbs through rainforest for 1km. Eventually the track levels out and then descends into open eucalypt forest. After about 2.5km you reach the 'Postman's Tree', a large, old tree with a hollow trunk that serves as an ideal place for a shady break.

Just before the Nightcap Bluff Lookout is a three-way junction. Keep right. A few metres beyond the junction is an undefined track to the left. Take this track out to an exposed rocky knoll that offers views to the southeast into Huonbrook and northwest into Doon Doon.

To return, retrace your steps from the knoll and back to the three-way junction. Turn left to walk back along the Historic Nightcap Track. Turn left at the fork with Gibbergunyah Range Rd and continue straight onto Peates Mountain Rd at the four-way junction to return to Rummery Park Camping Area.

TERRAIN

Fire trail, single track, rugged terrain, some steep sections.

CHALLENGES

Muddy track and leeches after rain.

This is a long walk so bring plenty of water and food.

The rainforest gets dark quickly – leave enough daylight to complete.

GETTING THERE

See pg 120.

CAFÉS

Doma Café Federal, The Rosebank Store, Crystal Castle.

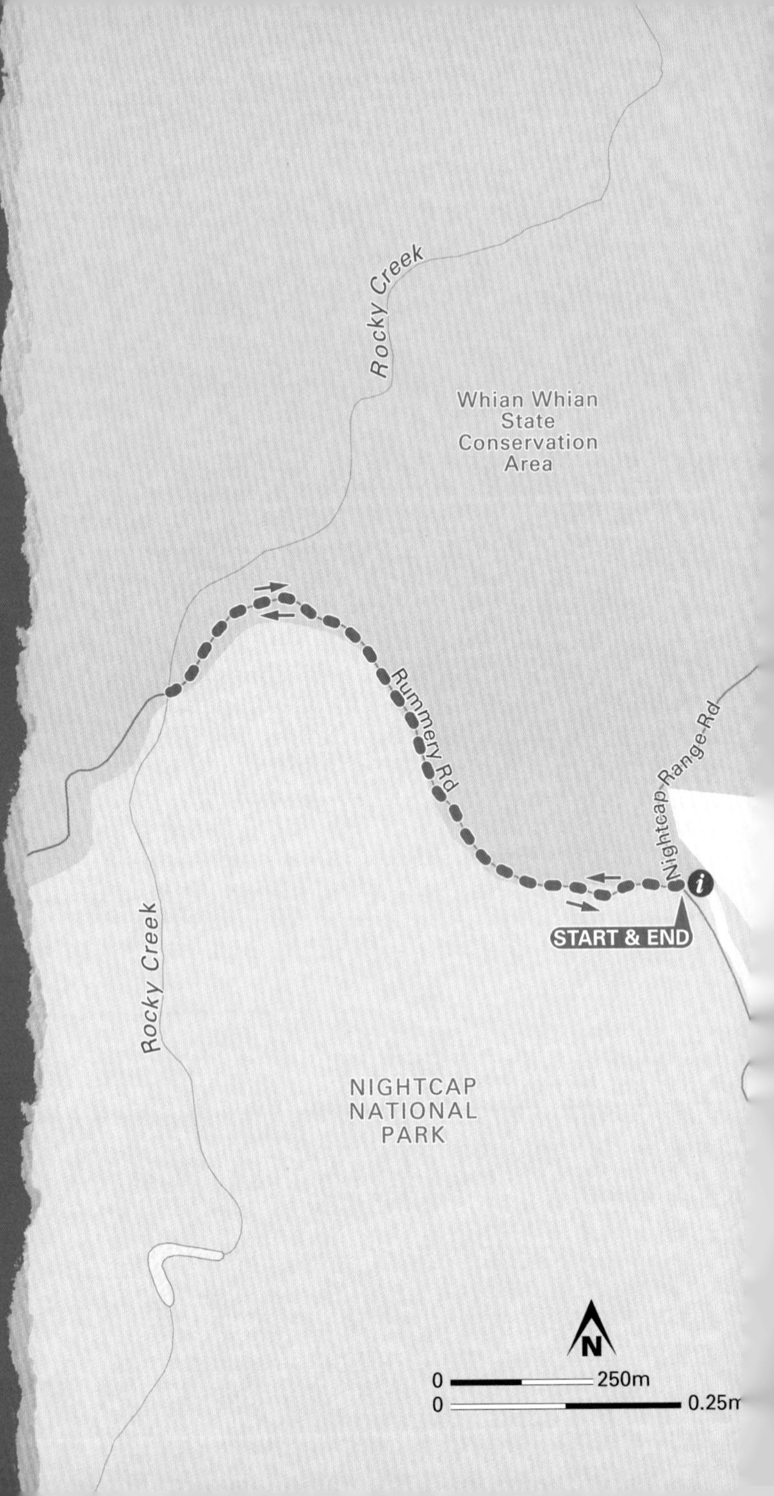

Rocky Creek

Whian Whian
State
Conservation
Area

Rummery Rd

Nightcap Range Rd

START & END

Rocky Creek

NIGHTCAP
NATIONAL
PARK

N

0 250m

0 0.25m

Closest Facilities: Rummery Park Camping Area

Peaceful creekscape. Beautiful rainforest walk. Further upstream is the Rocky Creek crossing on Blue Fig Rd. Walking shoes recommended.

TRAILHEAD: Information shelter on Nightcap Range Rd

From the information shelter cross Nightcap Range Rd to the start of Rummery Rd. Walk through the gate. The track descends steadily for 1.3km through stunning rainforest. The gully to the left is dominated by bangalow palm and blackbutt and makes for a picturesque forest walk. The sound of creek water greets you before you sight Rocky Creek. The rocks at the crossing are a lovely place to sit and take in the stillness of the creek and the reflection of the forest and the sky on the water. Allow plenty of time to relax and absorb the surroundings.

To return, retrace your steps along Rummery Rd. The track climbs steadily, taking you back to Nightcap Range Rd.

TERRAIN

Fire trail.

CHALLENGES

Muddy track and leeches after rain.

GETTING THERE

See pg 121.

CAFÉS

Doma Café Federal, The Rosebank Store, Crystal Castle.

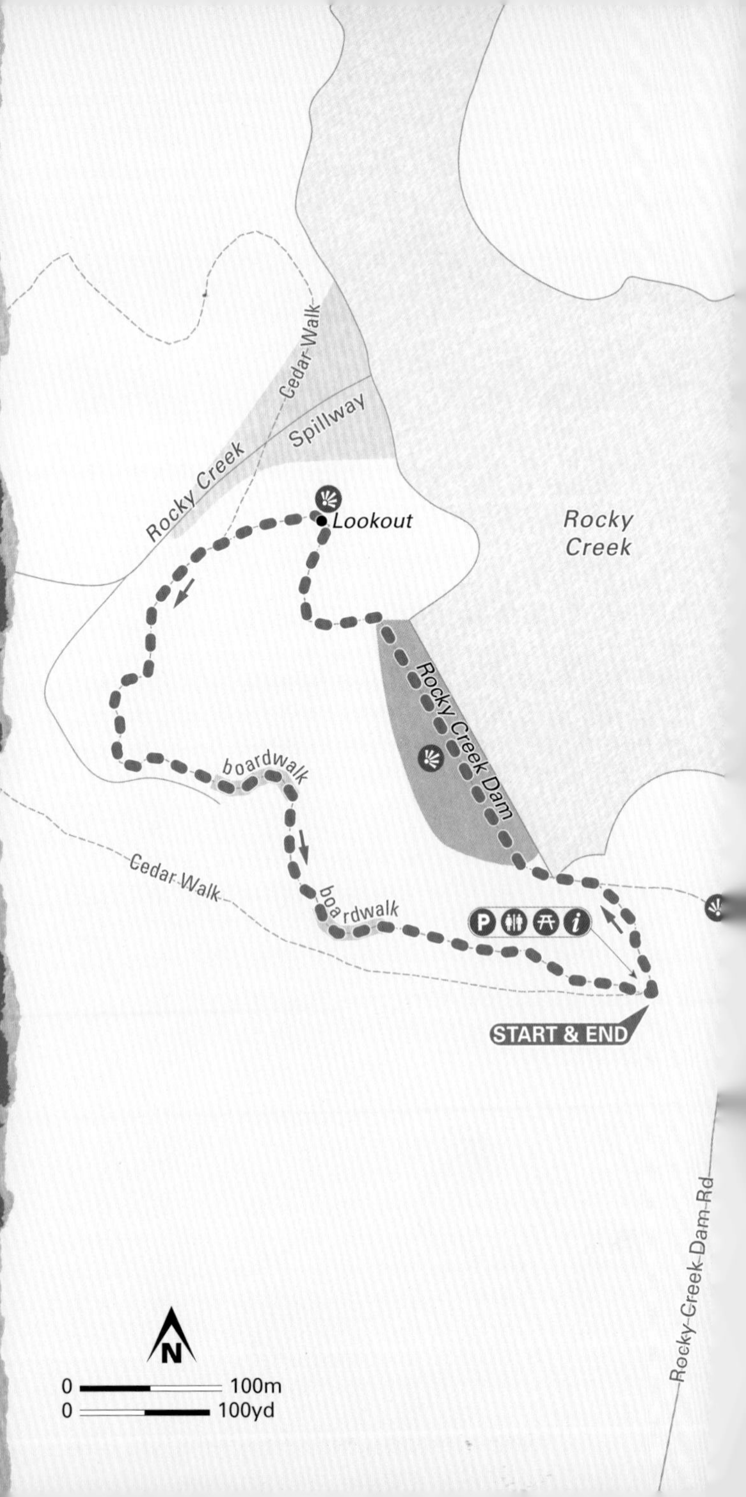

Platypus Boardwalk

Cedar Walk
Spillway
Rocky Creek
Lookout
Rocky Creek
Rocky Creek Dam
boardwalk
Cedar Walk
boardwalk
START & END
Rocky-Creek-Dam-Rd
N
0 100m
0 100yd

Family-friendly walk. Views over Rocky Creek lake. If you go early or late enough in the day and are very quiet you might just see a platypus. Signposted.

TRAILHEAD: Rocky Creek Dam picnic area

From the picnic area there are several pathways leading downhill towards the dam lake and dam wall. Cross the dam wall and follow the trail up to the viewing point overlooking the dam lake and spillway.

From there walk downhill keeping the fence on your right. Continue straight where the fence ends. The track eventually becomes boardwalk and takes you through lush rainforest alongside a pretty waterway.

Cross over the pontoon bridge and spend some time with the pretty water lillies. After the bridge turn left. Climb the shaded and grassy hill which takes you back to the picnic area.

TERRAIN

Boardwalk, grassy track.

GETTING THERE

See pg 121.

CAFÉS

Doma Café Federal, The Rosebank Store, Crystal Castle.

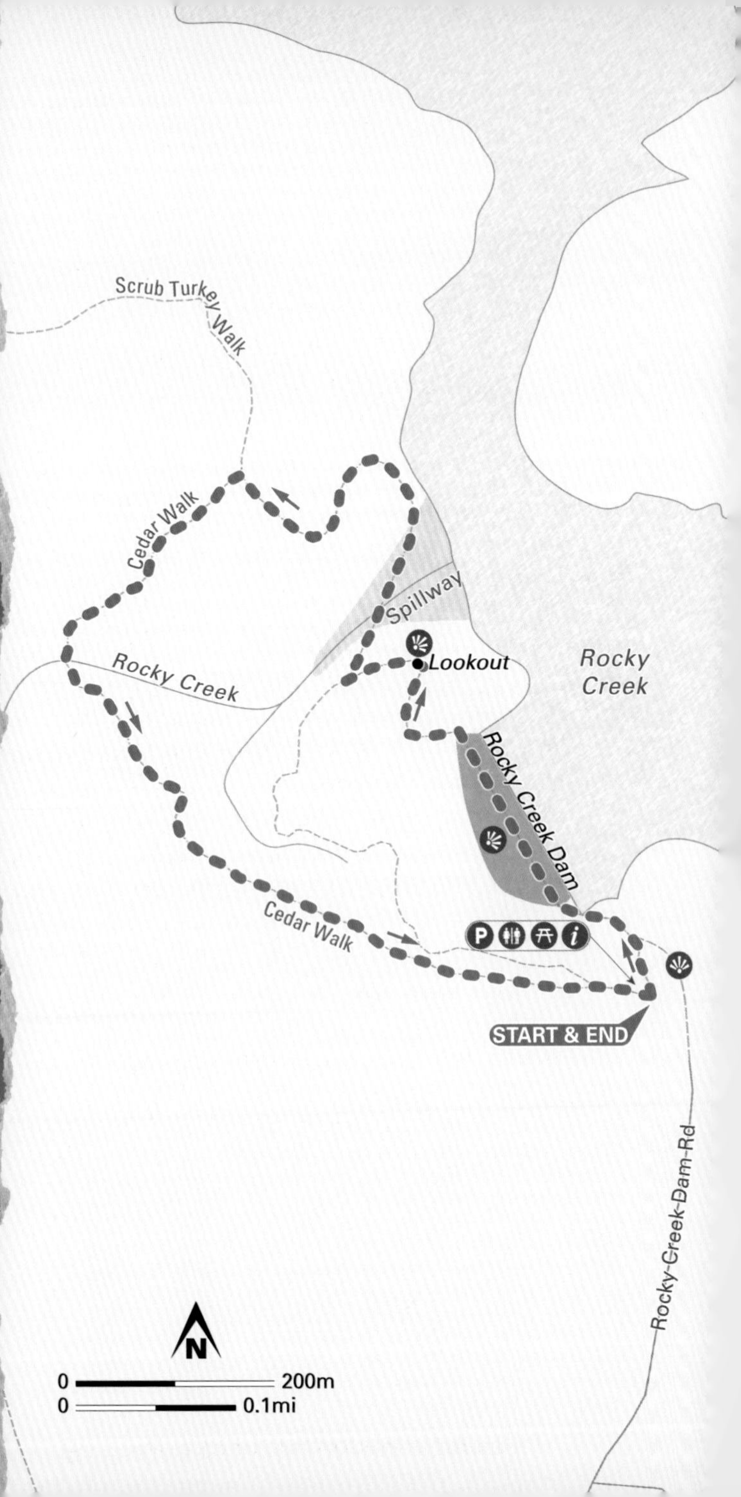
Scrub Turkey Walk
Cedar Walk
Spillway
Lookout
Rocky Creek
Rocky Creek
Rocky Creek Dam
Cedar Walk
START & END
Rocky-Creek-Dam-Rd
N
0 200m
0 0.1mi

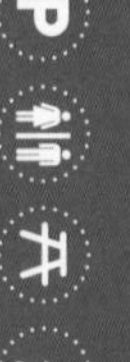

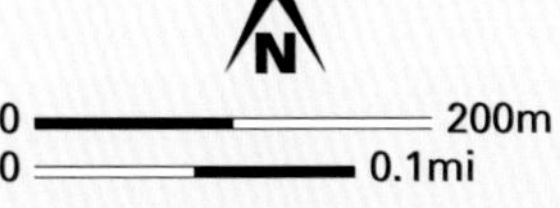

Family-friendly walk. Views over Rocky Creek lake. Signposted trail takes you through various stages of rainforest regeneration. Waterproof shoes recommended.

TRAILHEAD: Rocky Creek Dam picnic area

From the picnic area there are several pathways leading downhill towards the dam lake and dam wall. Cross the dam wall and follow the trail up to the viewing point overlooking the dam lake and spillway.

From there walk downhill keeping the fence on your right. Turn right at the end of the fence and walk across the spillway and into the Rous Water rainforest regeneration area.

About 150m after the spillway you will see a turn for the Scrub Turkey Walk on your right. Instead, keep to the left. The track descends to Rocky Creek, downstream of the dam. Cross over the creek and pick up the trail again on the far side. Now the trail climbs steadily passing the left turn for Platypus Walk, and takes you back to the Rocky Creek picnic area.

TERRAIN

Walking track.

CHALLENGES

Creek crossing – more challenging after lots of rain.

GETTING THERE

See pg 121.

CAFÉS

Doma Café Federal, The Rosebank Store, Crystal Castle.

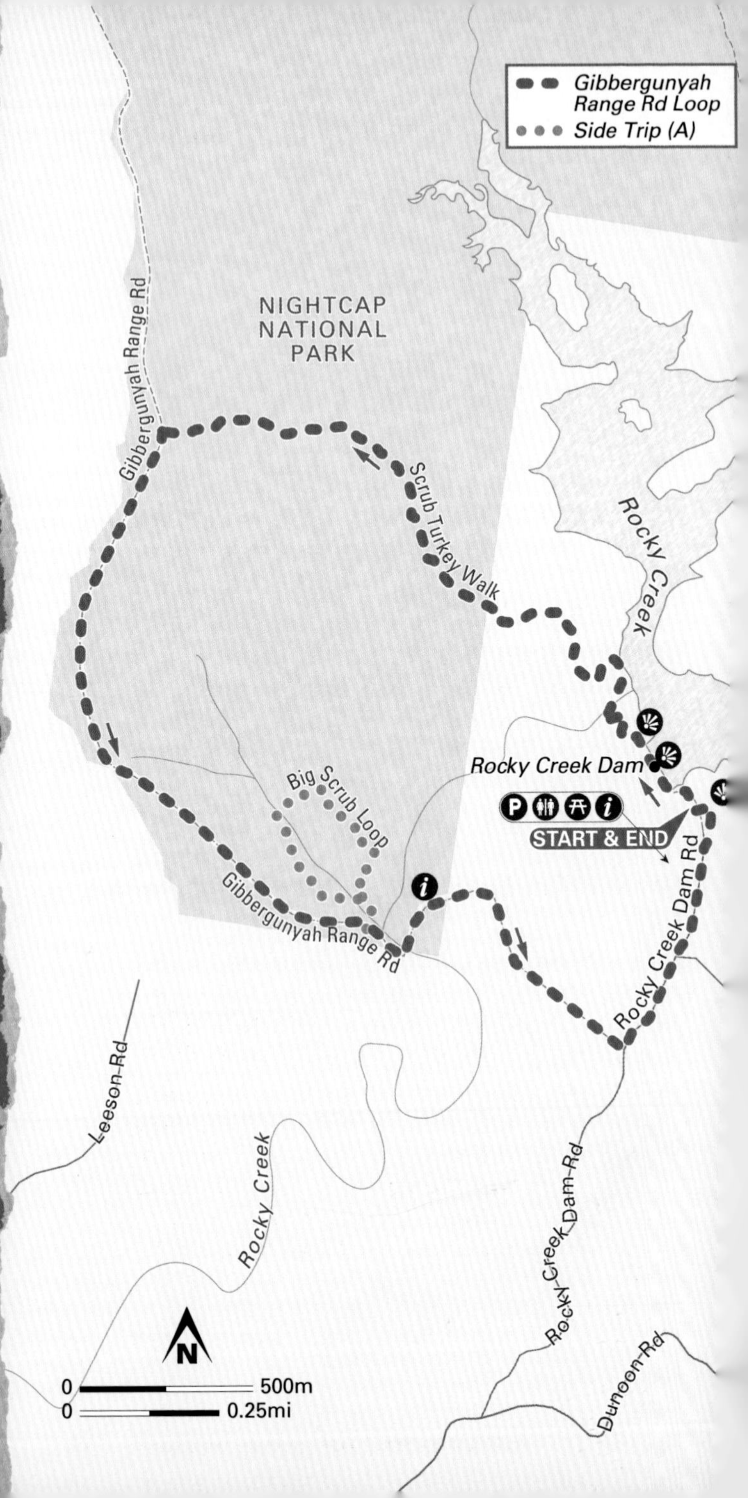

44

Gibbergunyah Range Road Loop

Gibbergunyah Range Rd Loop
Side Trip (A)

NIGHTCAP NATIONAL PARK

Gibbergunyah Range Rd
Scrub Turkey Walk
Rocky Creek
Big Scrub Loop
Rocky Creek Dam
START & END
Rocky Creek Dam Rd
Leeson Rd
Dunoon Rd
N
0 500m
0 0.25mi

This walk takes in the best of what Rocky Creek Dam has to offer. Waterproof shoes recommended.

TRAILHEAD: Rocky Creek Dam picnic area

From the picnic area walk to the dam wall. Cross the dam and climb to the viewing point overlooking the dam lake and spillway.

From there walk downhill along the fence. Turn right at the end of the fence and walk across the spillway into the Rous Water rainforest regeneration area.

About 150m after the spillway, turn right for the Scrub Turkey Walk. This quiet forest track meanders through mature forest for 2.2km and then reaches Gibbergunyah Range Rd. Turn left onto the road and walk south.

SIDE TRIP (A): ***After 2.3km you reach the Big Scrub Loop on the left, marked by a Nightcap National Park placard. It's easy to miss the track and the sign. This side trip adds a further 30 - 45 minutes to your walk.***

Continuing on Gibbergunyah Range Rd, cross the creek, walk through the national park boundary gate and follow the road. Once the national park ends so too does the shade of the forest. The remaining 1.4km to Rocky Creek Dam Rd is through cattle pasture. Turn left on Rocky Creek Dam Rd to return to the picnic area 850m to the north.

TERRAIN

Fire trail, forest track.

CHALLENGES

Creek crossings – more challenging after lots of rain.

Sun exposure in summer.

GETTING THERE

See pg 121.

CAFÉS

Doma Café Federal, The Rosebank Store, Crystal Castle.

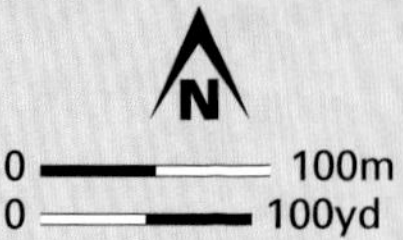

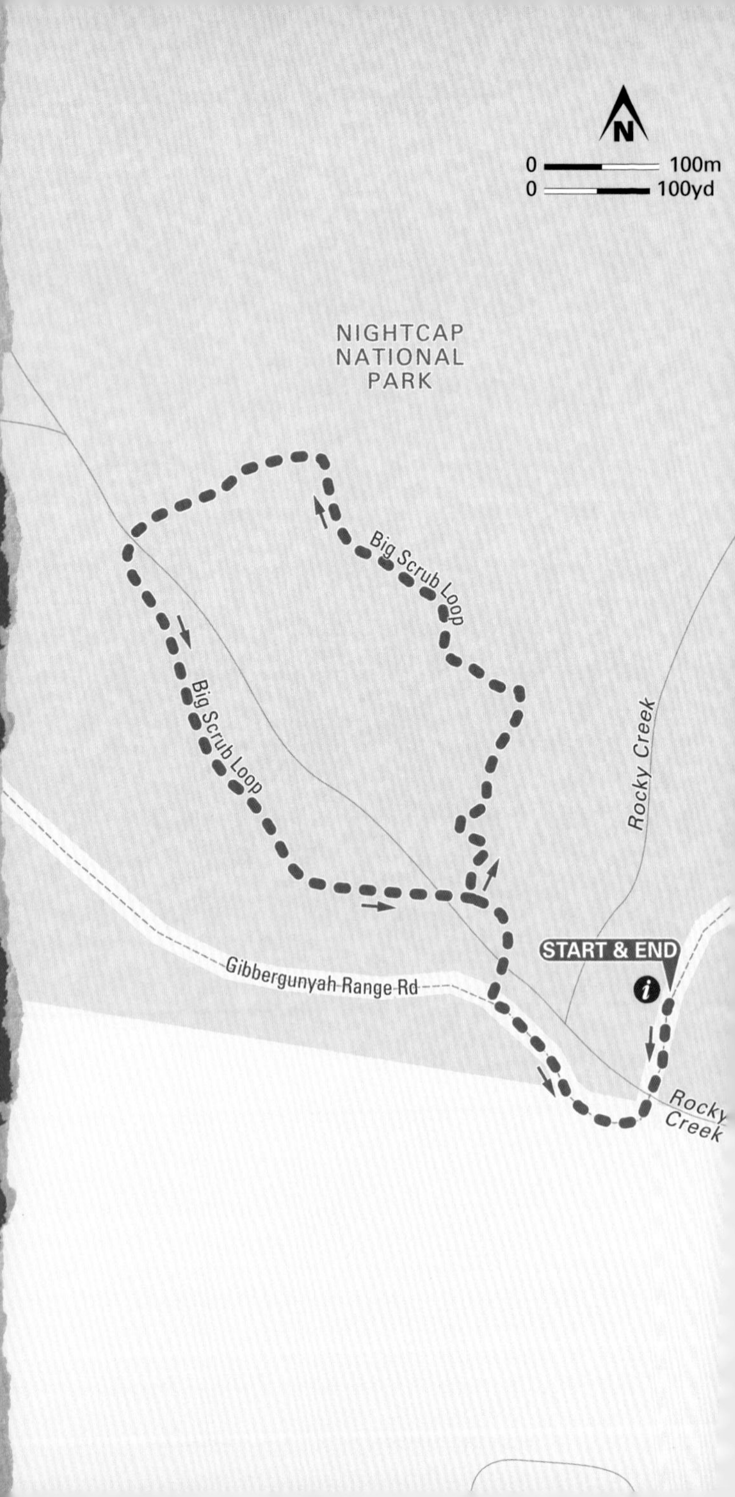
N
0 100m
0 100yd
NIGHTCAP NATIONAL PARK
Big Scrub Loop
Big Scrub Loop
Rocky Creek
Gibbergunyah Range Rd
START & END
Rocky Creek

Closest Facilities: Rocky Creek Dam Picnic Area

Ideal short walk for families and nature lovers. Signposted trail through one of the few remaining remnants of Big Scrub rainforest. Stunning old-growth forest rich with life. Best done slowly and quietly. Waterproof shoes recommended.

TRAILHEAD: Locked gate on Gibbergunyah Range Rd

Go through the gate and cross the creek. After about 200m you reach a small path to the right with a Nightcap National Park placard. This is easy to miss so watch out for it.

The path quickly splits in two. Keep to the right and follow the arrows. The track takes you through stunning rainforest full of large figs, abundant birdlife and crystal clear creeks and is easy to follow. The track eventually loops back on itself. Turn right at this point to return to Gibbergunyah Range Rd. When you re-emerge on Gibbergunyah Range Rd turn left and walk back to the gate.

TERRAIN

Fire trail, forest track.

CHALLENGES

Creek crossing – waterproof shoes recommended.

Wait-a-while vine and giant stinging tree (see pg 17).

GETTING THERE

From Rocky Creek Dam Rd (see pg 121) turn left onto Gibbergunyah Range Rd. Drive into Nightcap National Park to the locked gate.

CAFÉS

Doma Café Federal, The Rosebank Store.

P
Terania Creek
START & END
Terania Creek Rd
NIGHTCAP NATIONAL PARK
boardwalk
Bat Cave Creek
Protestors Falls
N
0 250m
0 0.1mi

Walk through World Heritage-listed rainforest. Ideal short walk for families and nature lovers. Going after rain ensures a full waterfall. Waterproof shoes recommended.

NOTE: This walk can be nice to combine with The Channon market.

TRAILHEAD: Terania Creek picnic area

From the car park walk back along the road you drove in by and across the creek crossing. You may have to wade through the creek water. The start of the walking track is on your left.

The first 250m of track is on boardwalk and travels alongside Bat Cave Creek through lush rainforest of bangalow palm, blue quandong and native tamarind. If you look up, a sheer cliff on the opposite bank of Bat Cave Creek is home to some beautiful ferns and mosses high in the forest canopy. Further along the track you will find yellow carabeen, strangler fig, red cedar and coachwoods. Rose-crowned fruit doves or barred cuckoo-shrikes are a possibility along this trail.

After crossing the creek via the wooden bridge, the trail becomes forest track and climbs gradually uphill to the base of the waterfall at the head of the U-shaped gorge.

Return by retracing your steps back to the picnic area.

Note: Don't swim in the pool below the falls as a small colony of the rare and threatened Fleay's barred frogs live in the area.

TERRAIN

Forest track, boardwalk.

CHALLENGES

Creek crossing.

Leeches possible.

Slippery rocks close to the falls.

The road into Protesters Falls area can get boggy after rain and the area can be closed due to flash flooding during, or after, heavy rains.

GETTING THERE

See pg 121.

CAFÉS

The Rosebank Store.

47

Mt Matheson Loop

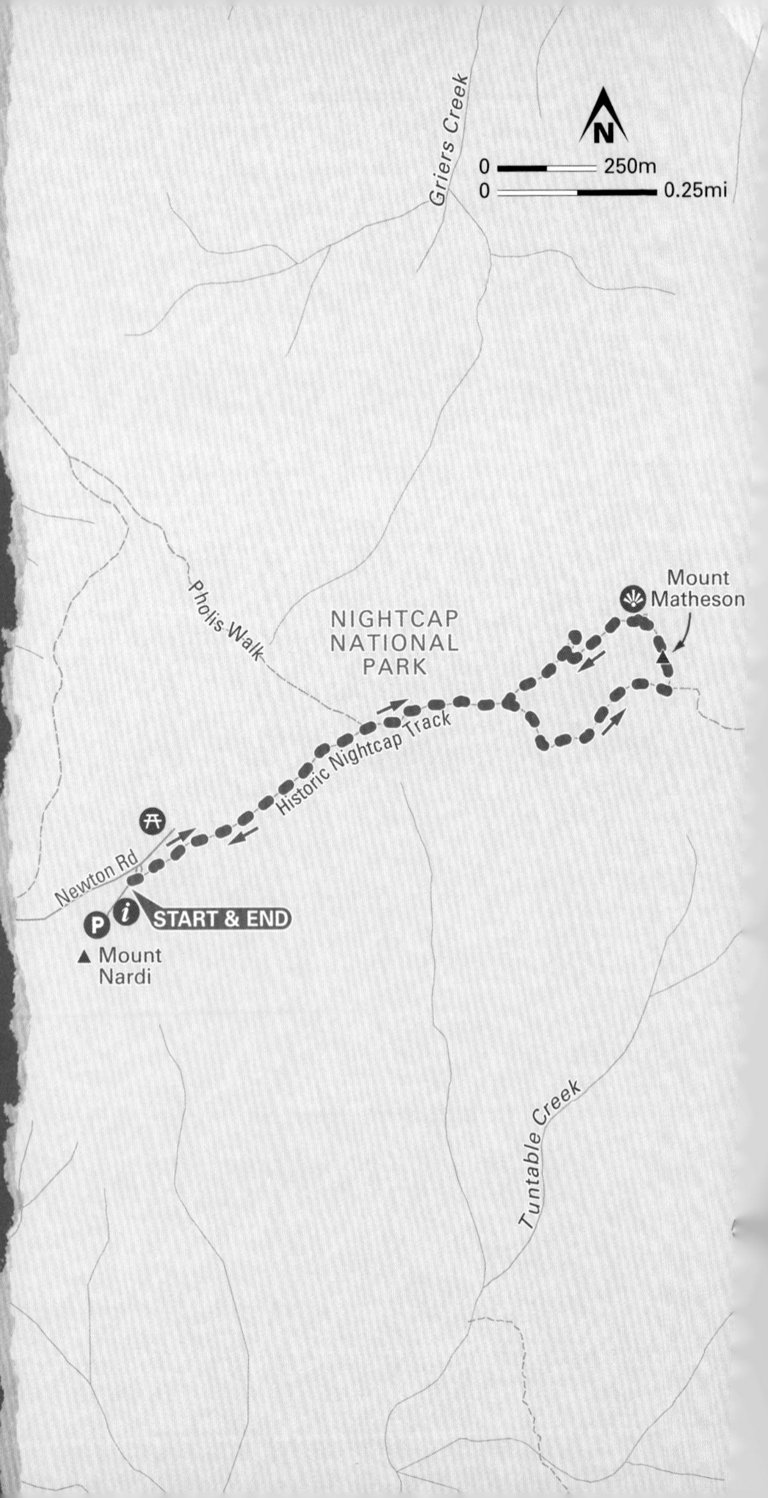
Griers Creek
N
0 250m
0 0.25mi
Pholis Walk
NIGHTCAP NATIONAL PARK
Mount Matheson
Historic Nightcap Track
Newton Rd
P
i
START & END
Mount Nardi
Tuntable Creek

Amazing World Heritage-listed, mossy, lush rainforests and valley-floor views. Winter means drier tracks. The 560m elevation provides a cool option in summer. Sturdy walking shoes needed.

Note: Can be combined with Pholis Gap Track

TRAILHEAD: Information shelter, Mt Nardi car park

The Mt Matheson Track starts beside the information shelter. Walk downhill through large groves of bangalow palms, tree ferns and buttressed trees. After 700m (10 mins) you reach the fork for Pholis Gap Track. Continue straight, and views of Wollumbin will open up to the north. In another 350m you reach the Mt Matheson Loop junction.

Take the track to the right. It ascends and crosses a gully via a small wooden bridge. Further along there is a turn-off to the right for the Historic Nightcap Track; keep left, heading to the northern side of Mt Matheson. Although there is no formal lookout you will see some spectacular views of the Doon Doon Valley floor as you walk along the northwest-facing slope. You will also notice the vegetation change. There are lots of beautiful, tall grass trees on this northern section of the loop track.

When you complete the loop turn right and rejoin your original track. Retrace your steps to reach Mt Nardi car park.

Alternatively you can extend your walk by taking the turn off for the Pholis Gap Track.

TERRAIN

Forest track, steps.

CHALLENGES

Leeches in wetter weather.

Sodden muddy tracks after heavy rain.

The rainforest gets dark quickly – leave enough daylight to complete.

GETTING THERE

See pg 121.

CAFÉS

The Rosebank Store

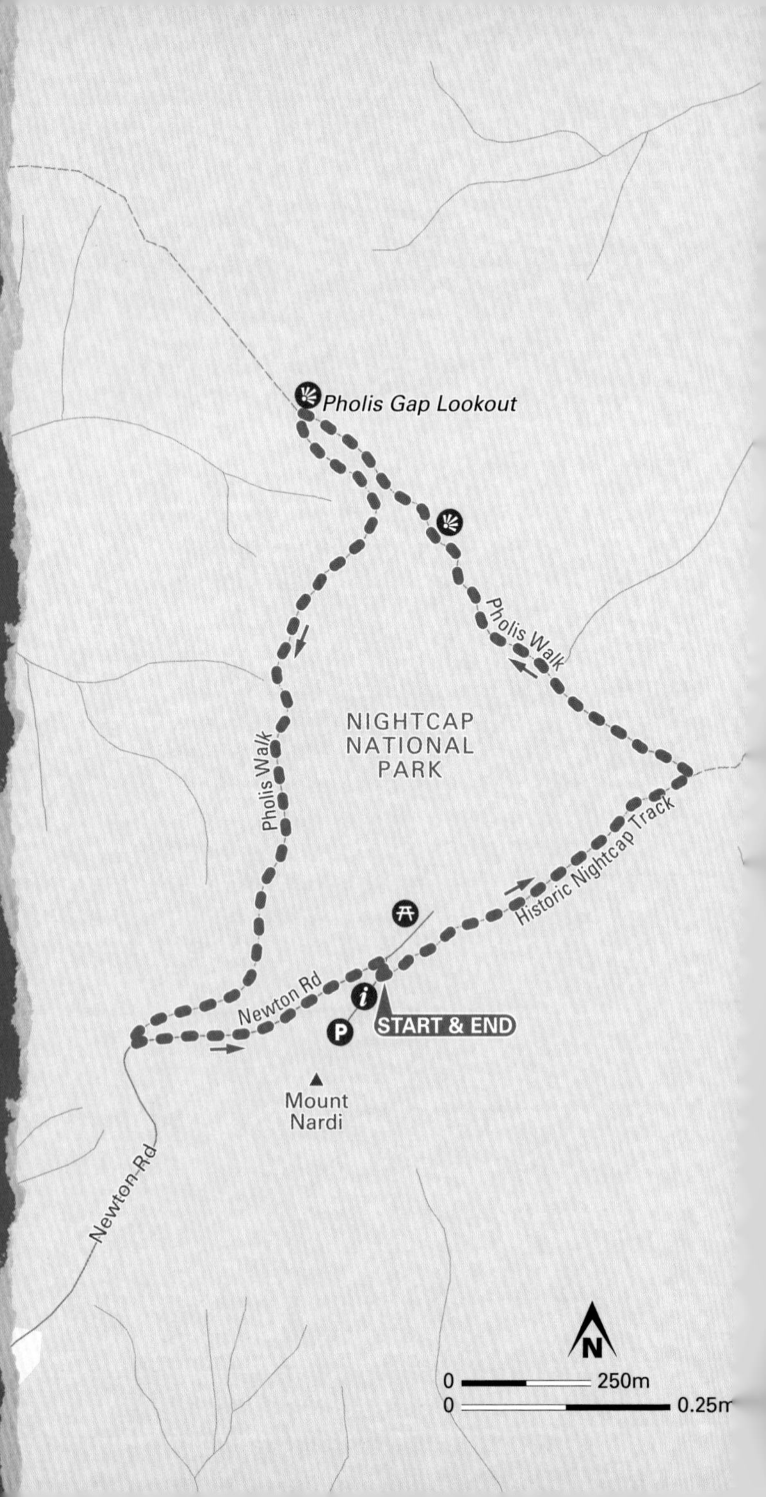

Pholis Gap Lookout

Pholis Walk

NIGHTCAP
NATIONAL
PARK

Pholis Walk

Historic Nightcap Track

Newton Rd

START & END

Mount
Nardi

Newton Rd

N

0 250m

0 0.25m

World Heritage-listed rainforests with huge tree hollows and views. Winter means drier tracks. The 560m elevation provides a cool option in summer. Sturdy walking shoes needed.

Note: Can be combined with Mt Matheson Loop

TRAILHEAD: Information, Mt Nardi car park

Take the track beside the information shelter. After 700m (10 mins) take the left turn for the Pholis Gap Track. The track descends rather rapidly towards the escarpment edge. This descent makes for easy walking and offers some excellent views of Doughboy Mountain and Jerusalem Mountain to the northeast, the Tweed and Doon Doon Valleys, and Springbrook Plateau 50km to the north. There are many huge trees with hollowed centres providing spots to rest and take in the views.

The informal lookout from Pholis Gap is slightly overgrown but offers spectacular views, including Wollumbin on the extreme left. The Griers Scrub rainforest is directly in front, with Doon Doon Valley beyond.

To return there are two options. (1) Retrace your steps along the Pholis Gap Track. (2) With your back to the old wooden sign, walk diagonally left and an overgrown old track should become apparent. This takes you through a logged but pretty rainforest and emerges on Newton Dr downhill from the car park. Turn left to complete the loop.

TRAIL

Forest track, steps.

CHALLENGES

Leeches in wetter weather.

Sodden muddy tracks after heavy rain.

Check yourself for ticks if you choose the overgrown track to return.

The rainforest gets dark quickly – leave enough daylight to complete.

GETTING THERE

See pg 121.

CAFÉS

The Rosebank Store.

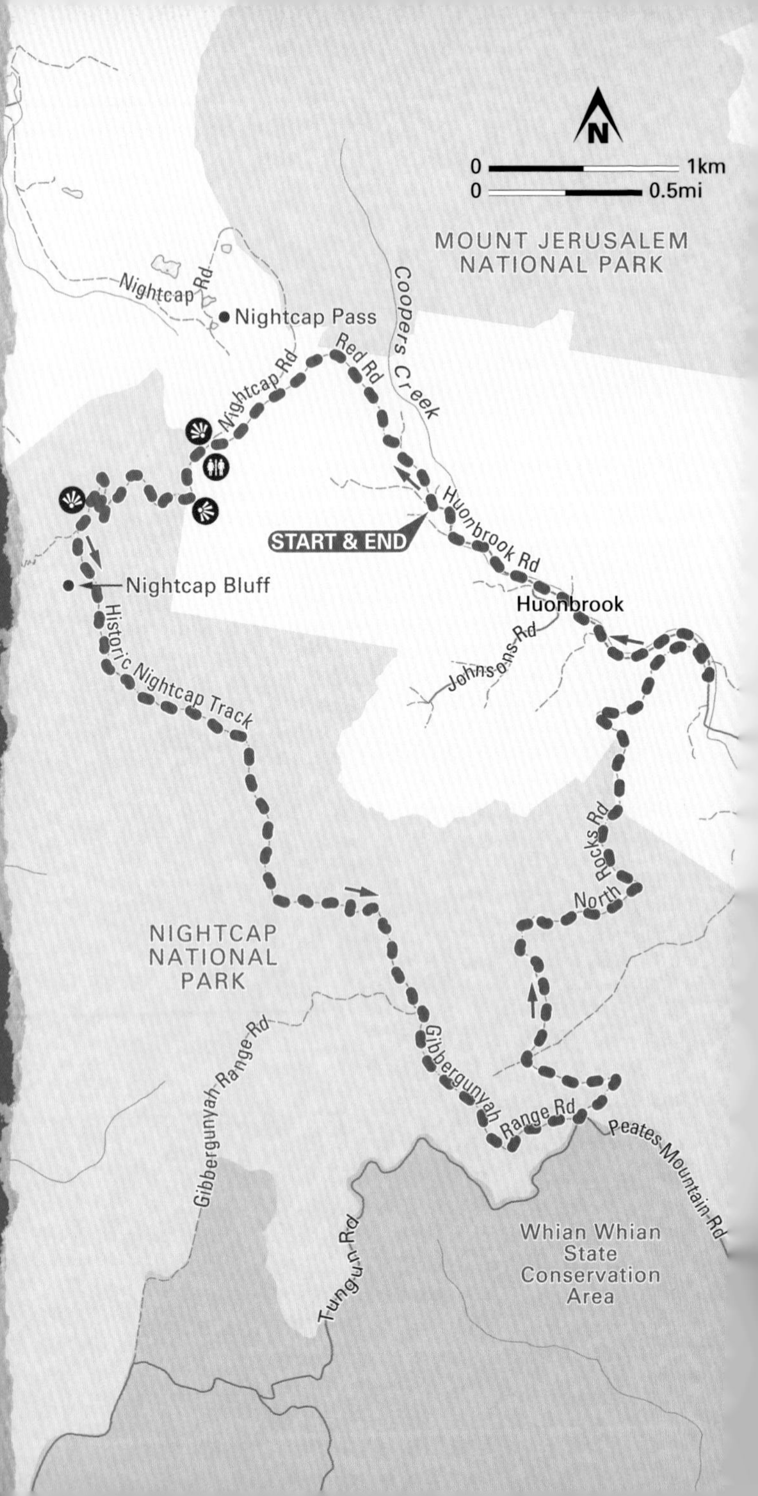

N
0 1km
0 0.5mi
MOUNT JERUSALEM NATIONAL PARK
Nightcap Rd
Nightcap Pass
Coopers Creek
Red Rd
Nightcap Rd
START & END
Huonbrook Rd
Nightcap Bluff
Huonbrook
Johnsons Rd
Historic Nightcap Track
North Rocks Rd
NIGHTCAP NATIONAL PARK
Gibbergunyah Range Rd
Gibbergunyah Range Rd
Peates Mountain Rd
Tungun Rd
Whian Whian State Conservation Area

Great views from Nightcap Bluff and Doon Doon Saddle. Spring brings wildflowers and orchids. Sturdy walking shoes needed.

Note: The first section of this walk is through private land along The Red Rd and the owners graciously allow access; please respect their property.

TRAILHEAD: Red Rd gate at end of Huonbrook Rd

Close the gate behind you. You are immediately faced with 1km of steep uphill climbing. After 350m keep left at the fork and walk through the gate. After a further 650m the track levels out and takes you through another gate to Doon Doon Saddle, which offers views to Wollumbin.

To the left of the toilets is the start of the Nightcap Track. 10 mins along this track a rocky ledge offers views down Huonbrook Valley to Cape Byron. From here the track climbs gradually for 1.5km to a junction on Nightcap Bluff. 30m before this is an undefined track to the right takes you to an exposed rocky knoll with views southeast into Huonbrook and northwest into Doon Doon.

At the junction mentioned turn left. The track climbs gradually along Nightcap Range past the large holllowed 'Postman's Tree'. The track reaches its highest point on Gibbergunyah Range and descends from here to Gibbergunyah Range Rd. Turn left. After 1.4km turn left at the four-way junction onto North Rocks Rd. This fire trail descends steadily for 4.1km and meets Huonbrook Rd. Turn left and walk for 1.6km to complete the loop.

TERRAIN

Fire trail, single track, some steep sections.

CHALLENGES

First section is steep and can be slippery and overgrown at times.

Walking stick recommended.

Best done in dry weather.

Leeches after rain.

GETTING THERE

See pg 121

CAFÉS

Mullumbimby cafés

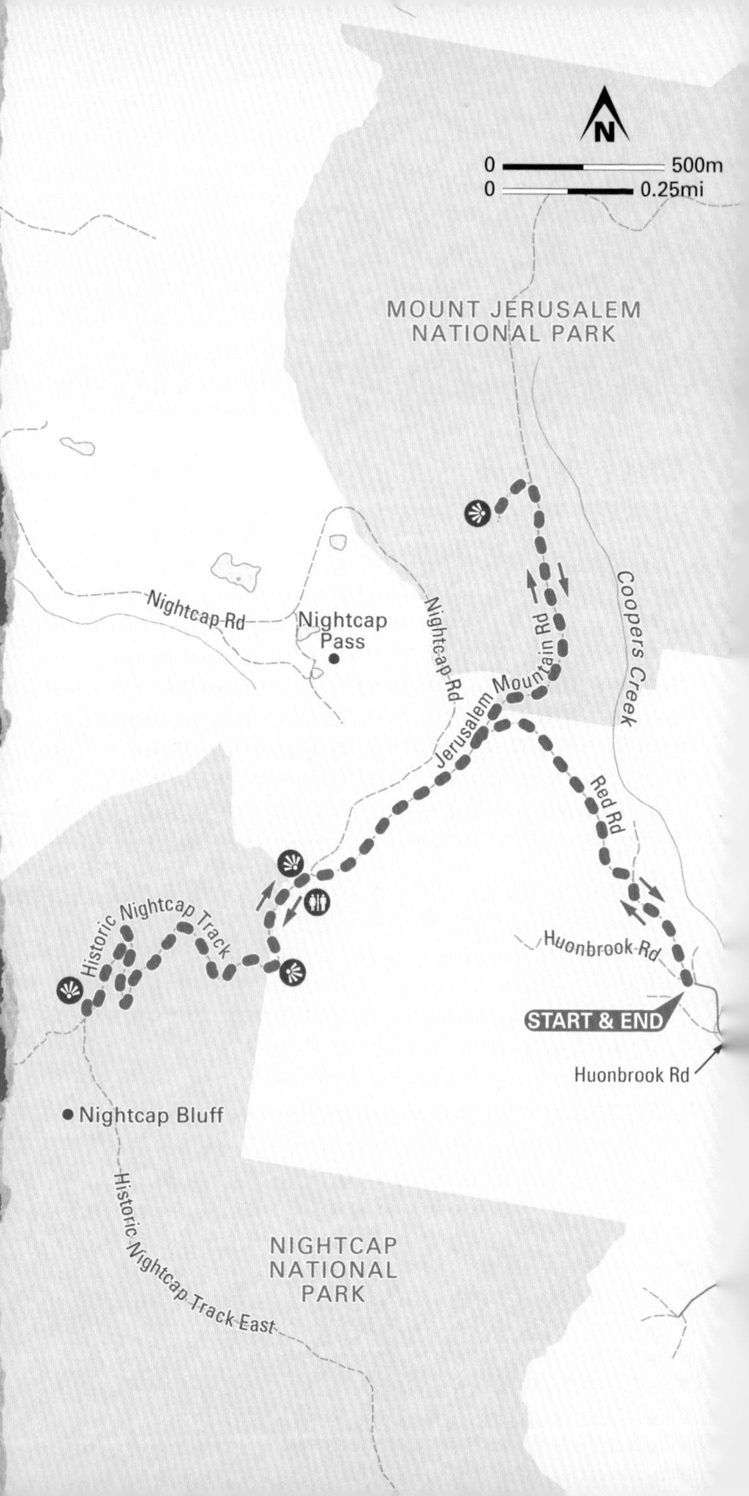

N
0 500m
0 0.25mi

MOUNT JERUSALEM NATIONAL PARK

Nightcap Rd
Nightcap Pass
Nightcap Rd
Jerusalem Mountain Rd
Coopers Creek
Red Rd
Historic Nightcap Track
Huonbrook Rd
START & END
Huonbrook Rd
Nightcap Bluff
Historic Nightcap Track East

NIGHTCAP NATIONAL PARK

Three stunning viewing places. Sturdy walking shoes needed.

Note: The first section of this walk is through private land along The Red Rd. The owners graciously allow access; please respect their property.

TRAILHEAD: Red Rd gate at end of Huonbrook Rd

Close the gate behind you. The road climbs steeply for 1km. Keep left at the first fork (through the gate). The track levels out and takes you through another gate to Doon Doon Saddle. Immediately after this gate take a sharp right onto Jerusalem Mountain Rd (easy to miss), through another gate, and uphill into Mt Jerusalem National Park.

As the path levels off it also widens significantly. At this point take the indistinct track to the left leading up to a knoll that offers stunning panoramic views.

Coming down from the knoll, turn right and walk downhill to Doon Doon Saddle ignoring the left fork to Red Rd. At the saddle clearing look for the Nightcap National Park sign. 10 mins along this track is a rocky ledge offering views down Huonbrook Valley to Cape Byron.

From here the track climbs gradually for almost 1.5km to a junction on Nightcap Bluff. 30m before this an undefined track to the right takes you to an exposed rocky knoll with views into Huonbrook and Doon Doon.

To return, retrace your steps to Doon Doon Saddle. Continue downhill keeping right after each gate.

TERRAIN

Fire trail, single track, some steep sections.

CHALLENGES

Red Rd is steep and can be slippery and overgrown at times.

Walking stick recommended.

Best done in dry weather.

Leeches after rain.

GETTING THERE

See pg 121.

CAFÉS

Mullumbimby cafés.

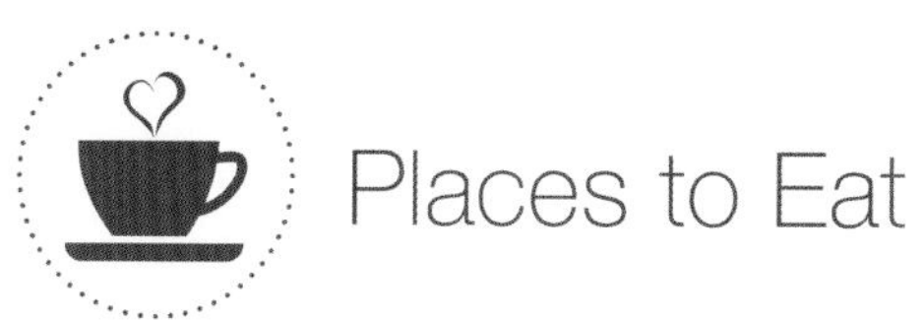

Places to Eat

BYRON COAST

Cape Byron Lighthouse Café

CAPE BYRON WALKING TRACK

9:00am–5:00pm daily • Cape Byron Lighthouse, Byron Bay

This small kiosk café possibly has the best view in Byron, spanning Byron Shire, Tweed Shire and Wollumbin. It has outdoor shaded seating, a limited range of off-the-shelf snacks, cold drinks, fresh coffees and teas. Cash only.

The Pass Café

CAPE BYRON WALKING TRACK

7:00am–4:00pm daily • Brooke Dr, Byron Bay

Nestled in the trees between Palm Valley and The Pass beach, The Pass Café is a lovely place to have a quiet chai or meal. With a wide menu and reasonable prices, this is a little hidden treasure close to the beach.

The Beach Café

CAPE BYRON WALKING TRACK • ARAKWAL NATIONAL PARK LOOPS

7:30am–3:00pm Mon–Thurs; 7:30am–8:00pm Fri–Sun
Clarkes Beach, Lawson St, Byron Bay

Byron Beach Café is the only café/restaurant on Byron's main beach and so is usually very busy. People come for the spectacular view to the beach and the water but also for the fantastic food. Licensed.

Top Shop

CAPE BYRON WALKING TRACK • ARAKWAL NATIONAL PARK LOOPS

6:30am–4:00pm daily • 65 Carlyle Street, Byron Bay

This takeaway café serves an excellent range of healthy food, juices and

drinks. Seating inside and out is casual. Vibrant and busy, with a great vibe and friendly staff, this popular spot attracts surfers, walkers and pretty much everyone else.

The Roadhouse

ARAKWAL NATIONAL PARK LOOP – SHORT • THREE SISTERS & KINGS BEACH LOOP

6:30am–10:00pm Tue–Sun; 6:30am–3:00pm Mon • 6/142 Bangalow Rd, Byron Bay

The Roadhouse is a funky café/restaurant/bar that serves great food and amazing hot drinks, including a strange but very healthy turmeric milk. Licensed.

The Farm

TYAGARAH TO BRUNSWICK HEADS LOOP • TYAGARAH COASTAL HEATH LOOP

8:00am–4:00pm Mon–Thur; 8:00am–10:00pm Fri–Sun
11 Ewingsdale Rd, Ewingsdale

The Farm on the road into Byron has a whole lot of everything going on and is definitely worth a visit. Situated in the 86-acre green space is Three Blue Ducks, which serves up a unique farm-to-table dining experience. Licensed.

Harvest Café

THREE SISTERS & KINGS BEACH LOOP

8:00am–4:00pm Sun–Wed; 8:00am–9:00pm Thur–Sat
18–20 Old Pacific Highway, Newrybar

Gorgeous cosy café/restaurant with wooden floors, wooden verandahs, excellent food and great staff. Popular with locals and visitors alike and for good reason. Indoor and verandah seating. Licensed.

Yum Yum Tree Café

BILLINUDGEL NATURE RESERVE WALKS

7:30am–3:00pm daily; 6:00pm–10:00pm Fri–Sat • 50 River St, New Brighton

The relaxed Yum Yum Tree Café is beautifully situated alongside Marshall's Creek in New Brighton. It has ample outdoor seating, good food, raw cakes and live music on Sundays.

BRUNSWICK HEADS CAFÉS

TYAGARAH TO BRUNSWICK HEADS LOOP • BRUNSWICK HEADS COASTAL HEATH LOOP • BRUNSWICK HEADS RIVER WALK

Torakina Café

6:30am–4:00pm daily • 2 The Terrace, Brunswick Heads

Torakina Café is an indoor and outdoor café with a bright airy feel. Located just beside the bridge in Brunswick Heads it boasts good food and great service.

The Footbridge

6:30am–4:00pm Mon–Fri; 7:00am–4:00pm Sat–Sun • 1/14 The Terrace, Brunswick Heads

The Footbridge is a funky café with a great vibe. The menu is eclectic and always tasty. Excellent food is served by gorgeous staff. It has terrace seating as well as cosy booths, a communal table and street-side counter seating indoors.

The Terrace Espresso Bar

6:00am–5:00pm daily • 4/16 The Terrace, Brunswick Heads

This corner café is a popular morning spot. Friendly staff serve good food, fresh juices and great hot drinks.

Brunswick Heads Health Foods

8:30am-5:00pm Mon-Sat; 9:00am-4:00pm Sun • 2/20 Fingal St, Brunswick Heads

This health food shop is also a vegetarian café that serves pre-made hot and cold food and cakes. All dietary requirements catered to.

BYRON HINTERLAND & NIGHTCAP NATIONAL PARK

GOONENGERRY NATIONAL PARK WALKS • NIGHTCAP NATIONAL PARK WALKS

Crystal Castle

10:00am–5:00pm daily • 81 Monet Dr, Mullumbimby

Crystal Castle is really a whole experience that deserves a few hours. It

has beautiful tropical landscaped gardens full of crystals, exotic plants and statues as well as a world-peace stupa. Their café overlooks the gardens and serves vegetarian food. There is also a vibrant bookshop and crystal shop. Various tarot and therapy sessions are available. If you just want food after your walk, however, this may not be the ideal option as there is an entrance fee.

Doma

7:30am–2:30pm Mon–Fri; 7:30am–3:00pm Sat–Sun • 3–6 Albert St, Federal

This is a special find in the Byron hinterland. Federal itself is a cute little village and Doma Café is a very cute café, the only café in fact in Federal. As it is Japanese run and in the heart of Byron Shire, you can get excellent sushi, or chai and a gluten-free brownie. Indoor and outdoor garden seating. Traditional Japanese doma room inside.

The Rosebank Store

8:00am–3:00pm Sat–Sun • 546 Rosebank Rd, Rosebank

The Rosebank Store is a little haven in the middle of the hinterland. Originally a general store, this eclectic and cosy café is attached to the E Fox Gallery, which runs regular exhibitions. The food is amazing and fresh with mostly organic ingredients.

MULLUMBIMBY CAFÉS

KOONYUM RANGE LOOP • RAYNERS TRACK LOOP • JERUSALEM MOUNTAIN • HISTORIC NIGHTCAP TRACK • NIGHTCAP & JERUSALEM LOOKOUTS

Empire Café

11:00am–4:00pm & 6:00pm-8:30pm Mon-Fri; 10:00am–3:00pm & 6:00pm-8:30pm Sat-Sun • 20 Burringbar St, Mullumbimby

Empire Café specialises in burgers and has some nice raw treats. Indoor and street seating.

Poinciana Café

8:00am–4:00pm Mon–Sat; 8:00am–7:00pm Sun • 55 Station St, Mullumbimby

Poinciana Café *is* Mullumbimby. The beautiful poinciana tree that sits

in the middle of the café gives it its name. This is a great laid-back hangout spot with lots of indoor and outdoor seating.

Rock & Roll Coffee Company

7:30am–4:00pm Mon, Tue and Sun 7:30am–9:30pm Wed–Sat
3/55 Burringbar St, Mullumbimby

Hidden café with cosy corners, wide range of food and lovely staff. Indoor-outdoor laneway seating throughout.

The Other Joint

8:00am–4:00pm Mon–Fri; 9:00am–2:00pm Sat
72A Burringbar St, Mullumbimby

Good food, friendly staff. The café is open during the day and the restaurant next door at night. Seating indoors and in the extended garden area out the back.

LENNOX HEAD CAFÉS

LAKE AINSWORTH TO LENNOX HEADLAND • LENNOX HEAD TO EAST BALLINA • EAST BALLINA TO FLAT ROCK

Foam

11:00am–11:00pm Wed–Thur; 7:30am–11:00pm Fri–Sat; 7:30am–4:00pm Sun
41 Pacific Pde, Lennox Head

Excellent food and service, house-made breads. Overlooks Seven Mile Beach so gets a nice sea breeze. Licensed.

Café Marius

7:00am–2:00pm daily • Swell Arcade, 90–92 Ballina St, Lennox Head

Great food, great chai and excellent coffee in a nice location. Helpful, friendly staff. Licensed.

Lime Café

7:00am–3:00pm daily • 70 Ballina St, Lennox Head

Prompt service and friendly vibe. Good value, tasty food. Special dietary requirements catered for.

Groovers Café & Restaurant

7:30am–3:00pm Sun–Thur; 7:30am–10:00pm Fri–Sat
63–65 Ballina St, Lennox Head

Good fresh food and friendly service. Special dietary requirements catered for. Licensed.

EAST BALLINA CAFÉS

LENNOX HEAD TO EAST BALLINA • EAST BALLINA TO FLAT ROCK • SHAWS BAY LOOP

Lighthouse Beach Café

7:30am–3:00pm Mon–Wed; 7:30am–late Thur–Sat; 7:30am–6:00pm Sun
Lighthouse Pde, East Ballina

Typical Aussie fare served by friendly staff. The main attraction is the beautiful view over Lighthouse Beach. Licensed.

The Belle General

Open 8:00am–3:00pm daily • 12 Shelly Beach Rd, East Ballina

This trendy, popular beachside café serves reasonably priced, delicious food. Special dietary requirements catered for including vegetarian and vegan. They also do fantastic raw cakes. Great service.

TWEED COAST CAFÉS

Corner Stop Espresso Bar

POTTSVILLE EUCALYPTUS LOOP • BILLINUDGEL NATURE RESERVE WALK – NORTH

7:30am–4:30pm daily • 6/1 Coronation Ave, Pottsville

This trendy little café is tucked away beside the tennis courts in Pottsville. Nice decor, good food, quality teas and coffees served by professional staff. They even have some raw treats. Dietary requirements catered to. Indoor and outdoor shaded seating.

Coastal Visions Photography Gallery & Café

NORRIES HEAD LOOP • CABARITA BUSH TUCKER LOOP

8:00am–4:00pm Tue–Sun • 2/2 Pandanus Pde, Cabarita Beach

Nice gallery café serving snacks and coffees. Invigorating surf art gives you something to feast your eyes on while sipping your latte.

Marty's at Caba

NORRIES HEAD LOOP • CABARITA BUSH TUCKER LOOP

4:30pm–late Tue–Sat; 12:00pm–late Sun
1/35 Tweed Coast Rd, Cabarita Beach

Marty's has a great vibe, with indoor and outdoor seating, a replace for winter warmth and cool summer sea breezes. It's a great spot for a beer and some food after an early evening walk (serves Byron craft beer Stone & Wood), and has live music four nights a week.

The fancy font on the street signage is hard to read, so if you find yourself struggling to make out the name you've arrived at the right place!

You & Bamboo

NORRIES HEAD LOOP • CABARITA BUSH TUCKER LOOP

8:30am–5:30pm Mon–Sat; 10:00am–5:00pm Sun
39 Tweed Coast Rd, Cabarita Beach

You & Bamboo is a bamboo clothing store with a rustic café. Gluten free and vegan options as well as raw treats. You can have your coffee or chai with home-made cashew milk! Street seating.

Sheoak Shack

FINGAL HEAD CAUSEWAY & LIGHTHOUSE • UKEREBAGH WALK-ON-WATER LOOP

11:00am–5:00pm Wed–Thur; 11:00am–10:30pm Fri–Sat; 9:30am–5:00pm Sun
64 Fingal Rd, Fingal Head

This groovy gallery-café is located on the banks of the Tweed River, under the shade of a she-oak tree. It's a relaxed coffee shop with friendly service and organic coffee. Live music on Saturday afternoons.

TWEED HINTERLAND CAFÉS

Main Arm General Store

HELL'S HOLE

7:00am–6:30pm Mon–Sat; 8:00am–6:30pm Sun • 491 Main Arm Rd, Main Arm

Main Arm General Store serves pre-made pies and hot drinks and has an outdoor seating area.

Flutterbies Cottage Café & Tyalgum Village

BRUMMIES LOOKOUT

8:30am–5:00pm Wed–Mon; 10:00am–3:00pm Tue • 23 Coolman St, Tyalgum

The word to describe Flutterbies Cottage Café is 'twee'. It was the town bakery back in 1926 and is now a flourishing café that attracts visitors with a penchant for cosy and frilly. Two cottages enclose a laneway that leads to a garden. All areas have seating. The café blends its own chai and has a coffee roaster and brewer on the premises. Generous, friendly staff. Licensed.Tyalgum village market happens on the fourth Saturday of the month. The Orpheum Bookshop next door sells hand-selected books and is beautifully decorated.

Mavis's Kitchen

WOLLUMBIN NATIONAL PARK WALK

Lunch Wed–Sun; dinner Fri–Sat • 64 Mt Warning Rd, Uki

Mavis's Kitchen is a treasure in the Tweed hinterland. This 62-acre property houses a bio-organic farm and stunning old Queenslander restaurant. Organic restaurant ingredients are harvested fresh every morning from the biodynamic kitchen garden or sourced locally. It's worth a walk around the beautifully kept gardens. Indoor and verandah seating. Licensed.

Rainforest Café

WOLLUMBIN NATIONAL PARK WALK

10:00am–4:00pm Thur–Fri; 8:30am–6:00pm Sat–Sun
134 Mt Warning Rd, Mt Warning

This is a laid-back café in a beautiful rainforest and creek setting. Indoor, outdoor and creekside seating.

Uki Café & Art Gallery

MT CHOWAN • WOLLUMBIN NATIONAL PARK WALK • CLARRIE HALL DAM • HELLS HOLE

8:00am–4:00pm Wed–Thur; 8:00am–10:00pm Fri; 8:00am–4:00pm Sat–Sun
1 Rowlands Creek Rd, Uki

A fantastic café that is beautifully situated, the Uki serves local coffee and a varied menu of fresh food that caters to all requirements. Indoor and verandah seating with views of the rainforest. Licenced. Serves Stone & Wood craft beer.

Tweed Gallery Café

BURRINGBAR RANGE TRAIL

9:00am–5:00pm Wed–Sun • 2 Mistral Rd, South Murwillumbah

The Tweed Gallery Café is attached to the Tweed Regional Gallery and Margaret Olley Art Centre. It serves a wide range of food as well as cakes, teas and coffees on its expansive deck. Dietary requirements catered to. Licenced café. The café and gallery both have a stunning view across the Tweed Valley. Admission to the gallery is free and it is generally quieter in the afternoon.

Moo Moo Roadhouse

BURRINGBAR RANGE TRAIL

7:00am–7:00pm Mon–Sun • 5886 Tweed Valley Way, Mooball

The Moo Moo Roadhouse serves typical roadhouse fare but has an interesting Old Moo Moo Speed Shop attached to it, which showcases some old cars, newer bikes and lots of vintage memorabilia. If you have refined tastes or dietary limitations keep driving. However if machinery and motorbikes are your thing then this is a great place to stop for a cuppa. The menu even has burgers named after bike brands and models.

Burringbar General Store

BURRINGBAR RANGE TRAIL

7:00am–6:00pm Mon–Sat; 8:00am–5:30pm Sun • 27 Broadway, Burringbar

Burringbar General Store sits across the street from the pretty Masterson Park and serves teas and coffees as well as pies and cakes. It has outdoor deck seating.

OTHER THINGS TO DO

- LAND
- SEA
- AIR
- GENERAL

Byron Bay Surf & Bike Hire **www.byronbaysurfandbikehire.com.au**	Bike Rental	1/31 Lawson St, Byron Bay
Vision Walks Eco Tours **www.visionwalks.com**	Guided Walks	Byron Bay
Walk With Me: Aboriginal Walk and Talk **www.nationalparks.nsw.gov.au**	Guided Walks	Byron Bay
Mountain Bike Day Tours **www.mountainbiketours.com.au**	Mountain Biking	Byron Bay
Green Cauldron Tours **www.greencauldrontours.com**	Tours	Byron Bay
North Coast Tours **www.northcoasttours.com.au**	Tours	Byron, Ballina, Lismore areas
Crystal Castle **www.crystalcastle.com.au**	Tourist Attraction	81 Monet Dr, Mullumbimby
Jay Carney is a local with a lot of knowledge of walking and cycling in the area. You'll find him at True Wheel Cycles, 19 Tincogan St, Mullumbimby or phone 0421 726 797.		
Byron Bay Dive Centre **www.byronbaydivecentre.com.au**	Diving	9 Marvell St, Byron Bay

Sundive Byron Bay **www.sundive.com.au**	Diving	9–11 Byron St Byron Bay
Brunswick Buccaneers **www.facebook.com/BrunswickBuccaneers**	Kayak Hire	Mullumbimby St Brunswick Heads
Cape Byron Kayak **www.capebyronkayaks.com**	Kayak Tours	Opposite 60 Lawson St Byron Bay
Go Sea Kayaks **www.goseakayakbyronbay.com.au**	Kayak Tours	Opposite 60 Lawson St Byron Bay
Byron Explora Stand Up Paddle **www.byronexplora.com.au**	Stand Up Paddle	21–23 Cemetery Rd Byron Bay
Byron Stand Up Paddle **www.byronstanduppaddle.com.au**	Stand Up Paddle	Byron Bay,
Blue Bay Whale Watching **www.bluebaywhalewatching.com.au**	Whale Watching	Brunswick Heads
Whale Watching Byron Bay **www.byronbaywhalewatching.com.au**	Whale Watching Byron Bay	9 Marvell St
Byron Airwaves Hang Gliding School **www.byronair.com**	Hang Gliding	Byron Bay
Pro Flyte Byron Bay Hang Gliding School **www.byron-lennoxhanggliding.com.au**	Hang Gliding	Byron Bay and Lennox Head
Byron Bay Visitor Centre **www.visitbyronbay.com**	Visitor Centre	80 Jonson St, Byron Bay
Brunswick Heads Visitor Information Centre **www.brunswickheads.org.au**	Visitor Centre	7 Park St, Brunswick Heads

BOOKS

Fox, Ian, Chapter 1: Geology. In Michael DeGood (Ed.), *The Fragile Edge*. (In preparation, 2016)

Keats, Norman Charles 1990, *Wollumbin*, NC Keats, Point Clare, NSW.

Louv, Richard 2012, *The Nature Principle: Reconnecting with Life in a Virtual Age*, Workman Publishing, New York.

Muir, John 1911, *My First Summer in the Sierra*, Houghton Mifflin, Boston.

Selhub, EM & Logan, AC 2012, *Your Brain on Nature: The Science of Nature's Influence on Your Health, Happiness, and Vitality*, John Wiley & Sons Canada, Mississauga, Ont.

Stetson, Nancy & Morrell, Penny 1999, 'Belonging: An Interview with Thomas Berry', *Parabola* 21: 26-31.

COMMUNITY DEVELOPMENT REPORTS

Duke, Anne 2012, 'Cabarita Beach/Bogangar Community Project Plans Report'. Report for the Cabarita Beach Bogangar Community Economic Development Committee. www.cabaritabeach.org

Trussell, Dianne 2007, Appendix F: 'Flora and fauna environmental assessment for Gondwana Sanctuary', 'Gondwana: Conversion to Community Title Development Application Report'. Report for Sustainable Futures Australia. www.gondwanasanctuary.org

PLAN OF MANAGEMENT AND VEGETATION MANAGEMENT DOCUMENTS

Cape Byron Trust 2002, *Cape Byron Headland Reserve Plan of Management*. www.environment.nsw.gov.au/parkmanagement/ParkManagementPlans.htm

Department of Environment and Conservation (NSW) National Parks and Wildlife Service 2004, *Arakwal National Park Plan of Management: Sacred Ancestral Place of the Byron Bay Arakwal People*. www.environment.nsw.gov.au/parkmanagement/ParkManagementPlans.htm

Department of Environment, Climate Change and Water (NSW) National Parks and Wildlife Service 2010, *Mooball National Park: Plan of Management.* www.environment.nsw.gov.au/parkmanagement/ParkManagementPlans.htm

Department of Environment, Climate Change and Water (NSW) National Parks and Wildlife Service 2010, *Whian Whian State Conservation Area Plan of Management*. www.environment.nsw.gov.au/parkmanagement/ParkManagementPlans.htm

Department of Land and Water Conservation 2011, *Ballina Coastal Reserve Plan of Management.* www.ballina.nsw.gov.au/cp_themes/default/page.asp?p=DOC-GEM-88-78-14

Environmental Training and Employment Inc 2004, *Sharps Beach to Shag Rock Vegetation Management Plan*. www.ballina.nsw.gov.au/cp_themes/default/page.asp?p=DOC-OJF-32-56-66

Environmental Training and Employment Inc 2006, *Lennox Point Vegetation Management Plan.* www.ballina.nsw.gov.au/cp_themes/default/page.asp?p=DOC-CHW-27-42-42

NSW National Parks and Wildlife Service 1998, *The Byron Coast Group of Nature Reserves (Incorporating Brunswick Heads, Tyagarah and Broken Head Nature Reserves) Plan of Management*. www.environment.nsw.gov.au/parkmanagement/ParkManagementPlans.htm

NSW National Parks and Wildlife Service 2000, *Billinudgel Nature Reserve: Plan of Management.* www.environment.nsw.gov.au/parkmanagement/ParkManagementPlans.htm

NSW National Parks and Wildlife Service 2004, *Parks & Reserves of the Tweed Caldera Plan of Management*. www.environment.nsw.gov.au/parkmanagement/ParkManagementPlans.htm

NSW National Parks and Wildlife Service 2012, *Broken Head Nature Reserve Draft Plan of Management*. http://www.environment.nsw.gov.au/resources/planmanagement/draft/20120911brokenheadnrdraft.pdf

SPONSOR WEBSITES

blk superwater:
www.getblk.com.au

Crystal Castle & Shambhala Gardens:
www.crystalcastle.com.au

Santos Organics:
www.santosorganics.com.au

The Bay Retreats:
www.thebayretreats.com

WEBSITE RESOURCES

Arakwal People of Byron Bay website:
www.arakwal.com.au

NSW National Parks and Wildlife Service website: www.nationalparks.nsw.gov.au

Office of Environment & Heritage website:
www.environment.nsw.gov.au

The Hamlet of Rosebank website:
www.rosebank.ws

Tweed Regional Museum website:
www.museum.tweed.nsw.gov.au

Photo Credits

ANDY THORPE
Page 18

DAMIEN TE WHIU
Page 135
www.gettyimages.com.au/galleries/photographers/damien_te_whiu

DAN MAHONY
Dan Mahony Photography: Pages 20 & 79
www.danmahonyphotography.com

DAVE HALL
Surf n Turf Images: Pages 30, 37, 39, 41, 43, 102, 107, 111 & 172
www.surfnturfimages.com.au

DAVE WHITEMAN
Dave Whiteman Photography: Page 97
www.davewhitemanphotography.com

MAIREAD CLEARY
Pages 17, 51, 53, 55, 63, 77, 81, 91, 93, 99, 113, 133, 139, 141, 155

MIKE DORAN
Mike Doran Photography: Page 86
www.mikedoranphotography.com

NATHAN HARRIS
Page 95
www.flickr.com/photos/n8from77

NOLAN WHITE
Nolan White Photography: Pages 6, 26 & 85
www.nolanwhitephotography.com

SAUL MORDAUNT
Saul Mordaunt Photography: Pages 19, 147 & 153
www.facebook.com/Saul.Mordaunt.Photography

SERA WRIGHT
Photography Byron Bay: Pages 16, 22, 114, 123, 125, 127, 129 & 151
photographybyronbay.com.au

SHUTTERSTOCK
Pages 9, 17, 18, 25, 45, 49, 71, 72, 83, 131, 137, 143, 145, 149, 157, 150 & 160

STEVE BACK
Steve Back Photography: Pages 1, 47, 56, 61, 65, 67 & 69
www.steveback.com.au

TONY WHITE
Tony F White Photography: Pages 10, 101, 109
www.tonyfwhitephotography.com

	LW	CB	RF	WRC	E	< 1	< 2	< 3	< 4	< 5	> 5	E	E-M	M	M-D
01															
02															
03															
04															
05															
06															
07															
08															
09															
10															
11															
12															
13															
14															
15															
16															
17															
18															
19															
20															
21															
22															
23															
24															
25															
26															
27															
28															
29															
30															
31															
32															
33															
34															
35															
36															
37															
38															
39															
40															
41															
42															
43															
44															
45															
46															
47															
48															
49															
50															